# SPIRITUAL FREEDOM

# SPIRITUAL FREEDOM

## GOD'S LIFE-CHANGING GIFT

Father Dave Pivonka, T.O.R.

PUBLISHED BY ST. ANTHONY MESSENGER PRESS
CINCINNATI, OHIO

Scripture texts in this work are taken from the *New American Bible with Revised New Testament and Revised Psalms* © 1991, 1986, 1970 by the Confraternity of Christian Doctrine, Washington, D.C., and are used by permission of the copyright owner. All rights reserved.

Quotes are taken from the English translation of the *Catechism of the Catholic Church* for the United States of America (indicated as *CCC*), 2nd ed. Copyright, 1997 by United States Catholic Conference— Libreria Editrice Vaticana.

Cover design by Jennifer Tibbits
Cover photo © www.istockphoto.com/Alexander Hafemann
Book design by Mark Sullivan

LIBRARY OF CONGRESS CATALOGING-IN-PUBLICATION DATA

Pivonka, Dave.
Spiritual freedom : God's life-changing gift / Dave Pivonka.
p. cm.
Includes bibliographical references.
ISBN 978-0-86716-860-0 (pbk. : alk. paper) 1. Liberty—Religious aspects—Catholic Church. I. Title.

BT810.3.P58 2008
233'.7—dc22

2007050943

ISBN: 978-0-86716-860-0
Copyright ©2008, Dave Pivonka. All rights reserved.

Published by Servant Books, an imprint of St. Anthony Messenger Press
28 W. Liberty St.
Cincinnati, OH 45202
www.ServantBooks.org

Printed in the United States of America
Printed on acid-free paper

08 09 10 11 12  5 4 3 2 1

# CONTENTS

THIS BOOK IS DEDICATED TO ALL THOSE WHO ARE IN BONDAGE AND long to be free. May you find what you are searching for, or, better yet, may what you are searching for find you. Be at peace: There is freedom.

It is also dedicated to the many people who have allowed me to walk with them to freedom. You know who you are. You have welcomed me into a sacred part of your heart and I am forever humbled by your trust and your love. You have taught me more about courage, persistence, honesty, love, hope and freedom than you will ever know. I told you more than once that God would use your story to bring others to freedom. I hope that this simple offering will do just that—help bring others to God's holy freedom. You will forever be remembered in my prayers and when I celebrate Mass. Be good and don't forget to laugh.

Finally, to all the members of my family, who have continually encouraged me and allowed me to live in freedom: I love you.

For this reason I kneel before the Father, from whom every family in heaven and on earth is named, that he may grant you in accord with the riches of his glory to be strengthened with power through his Spirit in the inner self, and that Christ may dwell in your hearts through faith; that you, rooted and grounded in love, may have strength to comprehend with all the holy ones what is the breadth and length and height and depth, and to know the love of Christ that surpasses knowledge, so that you may be filled with all the fullness of God.

Now to him who is able to accomplish far more than all we ask or imagine, by the power at work within us, to him be glory in the church and in Christ Jesus to all generations, forever and ever. Amen. (Ephesians 3:14–21)

THE FIRST THING SCRIPTURE TELLS US ABOUT FREEDOM IS SURPRISING, but faith sees this as wholly natural, since faith sheds a wonderful light on this question: *Freedom is a gift.* It is created by God, and this means that God wants me to be free. He has made us in such a way that we are free. If we reflect on this, we see that it involves a profound mystery. We are all creatures, and God has given us everything: our existence, our life and our freedom. Precisely this is the mystery: I am free, but this freedom makes me dependent. God has given it to me; I have not made myself free. To be creature means to be dependent, and perhaps our problem today (and throughout the modern period) consists in accepting dependence. We see dependence as the opposite of freedom, but when we read the Bible, we see that we are free precisely when we are dependent on God, as his creatures. Our freedom is not without ties; rather, it is a freedom that we receive as a task to be accomplished. Freedom is entrusted to me as something I must shape and take care of.

Our great models the saints show us something else. In them, we see the traces of a freedom greater than we had ever imagined, the freedom for which Christ has set us free. The *Catechism* says: "Freedom is the power to act or not to act, and so to perform deliberate acts of one's own. Freedom attains perfection in its acts when directed toward God, the sovereign Good" (*CCC*, 1744).

The greater my gift of myself to God and to his will, the greater my freedom. This is the heart of the biblical message. Jesus' entire life was oriented to the Father and to his will: "My food is to do the will of the one who sent me" (John 4:34). I invite you to join me in pondering this mystery: How is Jesus so independent and free, although he is completely dependent on the Father? We must surely say: He is so independent and free, not *although,* but *because* he is completely dependent on the Father.

This brings us to the difficulty that lies deepest in our hearts when we think about freedom, namely, the suspicion that I will renounce my freedom if I obey God, the suspicion that God does not really want me to be free. This suspicion is one of the fruits of the Fall. But the experience of the saints says something different: We become free when we trust God and his will and allow ourselves to be led completely by him. Look at Saint John Bosco—can one imagine a more spontaneous, cheerful or free person than Don Bosco? But what was the source of this freedom? It grew out of his total orientation to the will of the Father, because God gives us a share in his own divine freedom. And his freedom is endlessly creative and inventive. We see the same principle in Francis of Assisi, whose freedom grew out of his obedience to the Father and his love for Christ.

May Father Dave Pivonka's book on spiritual freedom encourage all readers to live their freedom as a gift, enabling them to give of themselves to the only one who can really give us the true fulfilment of our freedom.

*Cardinal Christoph Schönborn*
*Vienna, on the Feast of Our*
*Lady of Jerusalem,*
*November 21, 2007*

YOU CAN BE FREE.

The cry of the human heart, the cry of your soul, is to be *free*. Stop what you are doing. Listen. Go deeper. Can you hear it?

Let there be no doubt that the human person was created to be free. Take a moment and be still; be quiet. Listen to your heart, not your mind. You long to be free, and part of you in the very depths of your soul knows that what you are presently living in is not what God fully intended. God desires for you, for me, to be free. I have no doubt that you can be free.

I need to state that this belief is not fundamentally rooted in my confidence in you. Rather, it is rooted in my absolute confidence in Christ. Please, don't take this as a personal slight. It is just that I believe it is God who ultimately frees us; it is he who makes you and me freer.

I remember one time someone with whom I was praying said to me, "Father Dave, there were times that I did not believe I could be free, but I knew that you believed this, and at those times, that was enough for me."

You can be free. However, this is not going to happen by you simply repeating this mantra: "I can be free.... I can be free...." This is not a self-help book. If that is what you were looking for or hoping for, you may want to choose another book. (I must admit I do find it somewhat ironic that literally millions of people go the local bookstore to read another person's work on *self*-help.) Numerous other books may fulfill a desire for self-help, but this book is not one of them.

This book will provide a framework or a guide to help you come to a greater freedom in your spiritual life. However, since freedom, conversion and healing really are the work of God, it is he who will free, heal and restore you. This being the case, it is essential that you seek God. It is imperative that you pray. Time and time again, I am going to speak about your becoming still and quiet. Simply reading this book will not magically cause you to be free. Again, freedom is an act of God; he is the one who frees us. While I do believe this book can be a great asset, it is necessary for you to be present to God and allow him to break into your life in order to offer you freedom.

This is going to mean that you take time to pray. You must make yourself available to God. Stop, be still, be quiet and give God some space to show himself to you. My desire is that this book will help you in your prayer life and your interior life. I will continually encourage you to a greater interiority. This is radically different from self-help introspection. Introspection is simply you trying to figure out what is wrong—what the problem is—and then figuring out a way to fix it. Interiority requires you to stop and be still, asking God to show himself to you. It is asking *him* to reveal what is the problem or struggle, asking him to reveal what really binds you and then inviting *him* to bring healing and restoration. The difference between introspection and interiority is clear: One is led by you and actually ends with you, while the other is directed by God and in the end leads you back to God. I do not believe you are able to become fully free or healed on your own power. You must submit to the power of God.

Prayer is both an extremely natural thing and a somewhat foreign thing. We want to talk with God and, believe it or not, he wants to communicate with us. I recall a time when I told a group of university students that God wanted to speak to them. About a week later, a student barged into my office demanding to speak to me.

"You were right."

"About what?"

She went on to explain that when I had said that God wanted to speak with her that she thought I was crazy. However, she took up my challenge of praying daily for at least ten minutes. One day, she was floored.

"God spoke to me. He really did." She was giddy with excitement; she simply could not contain herself.

"Well, what did he say?"

"He told me I don't listen, and he's right, I don't! I don't listen to my mom; I don't really listen to my friends; and I don't listen to you in class. I just don't listen. Then God told me I need to listen."

Never before had I seen someone so excited at being reprimanded by God. But she had heard him speak and she was different because of it.

And so it will be with you. You need to take time each day to spend with God. I will deal more extensively with prayer later on, but for now, please take ten or fifteen minutes a day to reflect on what you are reading. At the end of each chapter, you will find a section that I have called "Journey to God's Heart." This is meant as a guide for you to help you pray and seek God as you read through this book. The "Journey to God's Heart" section is divided into three parts:

1. Listening—Simply taking some time to quiet yourself is essential to your spiritual life. There is a difference between "quiet" and "listening" and, to be honest, we don't do either very well. Often when we are trying to quiet ourselves and listen we get frustrated and start "doing" instead. Spiritual reading and other devotions are important, but don't do these to the exclusion of being quiet in order to listen. It is important that you be patient, trusting that God is going to speak to you. At first you may not recognize his voice, but in time you will come to know how he speaks to you and be able to hear him more clearly. Recall also that the Scriptures are God's Word and they are the normative way in which he speaks to us. Be patient when reading Scripture and ask God what he is trying to say to you through the Word.

2. Reflecting—What have you been reflecting on as you were reading? Hopefully the reading will raise questions

for you. Questions can tell you a lot about what you are thinking and feeling. Don't worry if you don't know the answers right away, just be patient and trust that in God's timing you will have a greater understanding of what God is trying to show you in your questions.

3. Conversing—This section allows you to begin to articulate what God is revealing to you through your silence, his Word and your personal reflections. I suggest you do this through journaling. I often journal because it helps me think more clearly. There is something very healthy about writing things down. My journals are not diaries, but rather my accounting of what I am saying to God and what I believe he is saying to me. Journaling also helps me to see what God has done and is doing in my life. I write about how I am coming to understand more fully who God is and who I am in relation to him.

While freedom is the work of God, it is always going to require effort by you. Your being still for a few minutes a day is not the only thing that will be required. To be really free takes work. I am going to challenge you to take a look at things in your life that you would prefer not to look at, to admit things you would rather not admit. This oftentimes proves to be very difficult. I am going to invite some of you to confront things that you have spent years trying to forget. This, too, will be very hard. (You can't say I did not warn you.) Do not be afraid; if you let him, God will lead. You don't have to go there by yourself. Again, this is about letting God lead and going where he goes. As long as he is leading wherever you go, he will be there with you. There is great comfort and freedom in this. It really is *his* work.

You need to make a decision regarding how badly you want it. How badly do you want to be free? Are you willing and able to do what it may require?

I am reminded what Pope John Paul II stated in a homily he gave at Lourdes on August 15, 2004:

> Our Lady of Lourdes has a message for everyone. Be men and women of freedom! But remember: human freedom is a freedom wounded by sin. It is a freedom which itself needs to be set free. Christ is its liberator; he is the one who "for freedom Christ has set us free" (cf. *Gal* 5:1).[1]

Our freedom has been compromised by sin and other very destructive elements. However, it has not been totally lost. God wants us to be free and "If God is for us, who can be against us?" (Romans 8:31). If you are willing, let us begin on the journey of freedom, which will lead us to the very heart of God.

## CHAPTER ONE

## FREEDOM IS

It was a first for me, I have to admit. I had only been a priest
for about nine months and was excited that I was still
experiencing firsts. My rookie season had been an amazing year and it was about to get better.

I was in Florida evangelizing on the beach with about
fifty students from Franciscan University. (Tough ministry, I know, but someone has to answer the call.) Laura,
one of the students, approached me and asked if I would
mind talking to a man she had met. I said I would be
happy to meet with him. As we walked to meet him, Laura
explained that she had first met the man the day before
and had begun talking with him. She had learned that the
man was Catholic and that he had a very checkered past.
He had lived most of his life up North and was in Florida
for drug rehabilitation at a facility a few blocks from the
beach. Laura had told him there was a priest available if
he wanted to talk, and after two offers, the man had
accepted.

I can still remember when I first saw "Ron." His skin was
a weathered, reddish-tan color. It looked tough, worn and

tired. It had been days since he had shaved. The little hair he did have was pulled back in a ponytail that reached the top of his shoulders. He was not wearing a shirt, and his upper body resembled a world map with different-sized tattoos calling to mind faded memories. One of his ears had several rings in it.

In contrast, I was dressed in a nice, clean, white T-shirt with a Christian symbol on the back, swim trunks and sandals. My skin was colorless and looked as if I had been hibernating for months, which was not far from the truth after a cold Ohio winter. It appeared that Ron and I had little in common. However, I too was losing my hair, so Ron and I did have one thing in common.

I was not sure what I had gotten myself into and wondered where this was going to lead. This was certainly going to be interesting. In seminary, we had been told that in the first six months of being a priest, we would hear everything. Well, in my case this was not true. For me, it took nine months.

Ron looked tired, as if he had been fighting too hard for too long. I really couldn't tell how old he was; he could have been thirty or he could have been fifty. He looked beaten. I remember his eyes—I always notice eyes. They were dark, bloodshot and distant, as if he were trying to remember something from his past.

When I first approached him, he was seated on a blanket. As Laura introduced us, Ron tried to "tidy" things up. He moved his suntan lotion bottle, his cigarettes, straightened his blanket and leveled the sand around him—anything to avoid prolonged eye contact. He reminded me of a nervous mother picking up the newspapers in her living room before inviting an unexpected guest to be seated. Eventually, I did sit down, and Ron and I began to talk. At first, we exchanged words about nothing: the weather, the beach and the ocean—small talk. Slowly, Ron began to relax, as did I, and we began to really talk.

Sheepishly, Ron started to share his story with me. Yes, he was in Florida for drug rehabilitation, and, yes, he'd been using drugs for "about twenty years...not sure exactly how long." He had been clean for four months, which was the longest period since he had first started using. He shared that he was beginning to believe that it may be possible to get "out from under this addiction."

Ron was born and raised Catholic, but he quit attending Mass about the same time he began using drugs. He thought he was about fifteen at that time, but he couldn't remember exactly.

Ron shared more of his story and soon he just began to talk, as I sat back and listened. At first his words were guarded, but eventually they flowed out from him as if the dam had finally been broken. Story after story gushed from his heart. It was if they had been jammed up for years, decades, and finally he was able to let them all out.

Ron had seen it all. He had done everything. He had robbed people, beaten people and spent time in prison. He had done more drugs than he could ever remember. He was sure he had hurt people who would never be able to forgive him. As Ron spoke, I could literally see burdens being lifted from him. Tears slowly developed in the corners of his eyes.

Then the tears broke free from his eyes and gently rolled down his cheeks. At the same time, a light began to flicker in his eyes. It was faint, but it was a light.

I began to feel the presence of God as he told one story after another. At one point, he looked at me through his tears and said, "Father, you want to know how bad it got? A few years ago, I had no place to live so I moved in with my mother. I remember she had just purchased a little puppy." Ron paused to catch his breath. "Father, I would put out my cigarettes on this little puppy." Tears ran down his cheeks. "Father, what kind of person would do that to a little puppy?" Tears ran down *my* cheeks. I prayed and rejoiced at what I could see God doing in Ron's life.

I began to talk to Ron about a God who loves passionately and without condition. I shared with him about a God who sent his only Son so that we may have life and about how Jesus forgives. "Ron, you really are loved. You can be forgiven."

As I spoke, Ron's eyes looked as if he were remembering something, something he had forgotten long ago. I shared with Ron that there was not a place in his heart that God could not shine his light and that this light would defeat the darkness.

"Light always wins. No matter how dark the darkness is, the smallest light always shatters the darkness. Ron, Jesus was raised out of darkness, he is light—and he *wins!*" I exclaimed, "You really can be new; Christ really can take things that are ugly and gross and change them."

After talking for a long time, I asked Ron if he wanted to go to confession. He stated that it had been over twenty-five years since he had gone to confession and wasn't sure if he remembered how. Encouragingly I said, "I can coach you." So we began. There on the sunny beach in Florida, I heard Ron's confession. My father is a physician and he probably got used to seeing people come back to life after nearly dying. But I was awed as I saw Ron literally come back to life before my very eyes. His eyes became brighter. He no longer looked so tired and worn. There was a peace about him. I began to pray with Ron, and I saw waves of grace flowing over him. I led Ron in a prayer of commitment to Jesus Christ and now he was no longer crying; he was beaming. "Jesus, come into my heart.... Forgive me.... I accept you as my Savior.... Fill me with your Holy Spirit.... Make me new.... Free me...."

Then I talked to Ron about going to Mass on Sunday. "I can *do* that? I get to go back to Mass?" He looked like a kid who had found out he was going to get to go to Disney World instead of having a tooth pulled.

Ron, for the first time in over twenty-five years, was free. He *experienced* the freedom. I got to watch a man who had been dead come back to life; I watched a man who had been a slave become free. Ron had been a slave to his past, his suffering, his addictions, his sin, his fear, a slave to himself and to countless other things. In one moment of time, God had broken into Ron's heart and in that moment he had experienced God's freeing power. Jesus had become real to him. He had broken into his life and had set him free. Jesus' words, referring to himself as the Son of God, are forever true: "So if a son frees you, then you will truly be free" (John 8:36).

Ron and I parted ways that day, and I never saw him again. I have no idea what became of his life, whether or not it was permanently changed. Perhaps three months later he was struggling with his old demons again, but on that day, on a beach in Florida, Ron tasted freedom.

### America: Home of the Free?

So, what is it? What is freedom? I think there are a lot of ideas out there about freedom that are not correct. Many people have a false understanding of freedom. Freedom is not simply the ability to do whatever one wants whenever one wants to do it. Freedom has to be more than the capability of a human person to pursue the next sensual pleasure without restriction. Freedom is also not merely political, being allowed to weigh in with your opinion and vote for your favorite candidate.

Freedom, of course, is a very common theme in the United States. We Americans talk a great deal about this thing called "freedom" and we will fight and die to maintain it. This ideal, New Hampshire's state motto, is expressed directly on its license plates: "Live Free or Die." The Founding Fathers who established this country believed in a man's right to be free. They founded the United States of America on the fundamental principles that man should be free: free to speak, free to publish, free to bear arms, free to worship. In other words, freedom is simply a part of the American DNA. As Americans, we are oriented toward freedom and much of the world sees it as one of our greatest attributes, which it is.

However, this type of freedom, while a blessing, is only

a *political* freedom. Freedom that has God as its source goes much deeper and is the most authentic freedom of all. Sadly, most Americans do not experience this deeper freedom. They do not even know it exists.

It is such a blessing to live in a country where we are free, but even in the midst of this freedom, many people experience tremendous bondage. It is true that we experience political freedom, the freedom to choose our leaders, the freedom to come and go as we please, the freedom to live where we want. But there is much more to freedom than this.

*So, What Is It?*

Great question. I am reminded of what Pope John Paul II said on this topic to a group of young people gathered in St. Louis during his 1999 pastoral visit:

> Do not be taken in by **false values and deceptive slogans**, especially about your freedom. True freedom is a wonderful gift from God, and it has been a cherished part of your country's history. But when freedom is separated from truth, individuals lose their moral direction and the very fabric of society begins to unravel.
>
> Freedom is not the ability to do anything we want, whenever we want. Rather, **freedom is the ability to live responsibly the truth of our relationship with God and with one another.** Remember what Jesus said: "you will know the truth and the truth will set you free" (Jn 8:32). Let no one mislead you or prevent you from seeing what really matters. Turn to Jesus, listen to him, and discover the true meaning and direction of your lives.[1]

This can often be difficult to hear. Many people believe that freedom actually does mean they are able to do whatever they want, whenever they want, without limits, boundaries or responsibility. "No one is going to tell me what to do."

Too many people really do think that the sole source of freedom comes from the government that exercises authority over them. But the freedom I am speaking of is not that kind of freedom. It is much deeper than that, more precious, more sacred, more holy. True freedom comes from the very nature of God. While a person can live in the freedom offered by a government, he or she can still be a slave. And while another may live in a war-torn, oppressed region such as Bosnia, that person can be truly free.

Take Michal, for example. He was living in the shadows of a terrible war. He had nothing, could not come and go as he pleased, and by all accounts would not be considered "free." It was 1998, and I was in Bosnia with signs of the recently ended war all around me. About forty of my students and I were spending a day at a refugee center which was an old psychiatric hospital now inhabited by people who had no other place to live because their homes and villages had been destroyed. This abandoned hospital was now their "home." They had no money and no means of transportation. Because of that, they were "prisoners" to this compound.

When I walked into Michal's "apartment" (which was actually a single room in the facility) his scar-ridden face was beaming. His smile, though checkered with missing teeth, filled the room with a graced sense of joy and welcome. He and his wife quickly began waiting on us (me and a few students). They offered to split a couple of cookies and a single beer with us. These were precious luxuries that Michal had been saving for a time such as this. We began to talk but soon it became obvious that speech was difficult for Michal, so his wife recounted their story.

During the war, she told us, soldiers had broken into their home and forced Michal outside where they bound his hands behind his back with barbed wire. Then they proceeded to beat him, and they slit his throat and left him for dead. The soldiers went back into the house and forced Michal's wife into the back of a truck. From there, they went from house to house beating people and destroying their homes. As the soldiers and prisoners left the village, they came across a badly beaten man crawling across the road. The man was thrown into the back of the truck. He had been beaten beyond recognition; Michal's wife was unable to recognize her own husband lying at her feet.

Occasionally, as his wife recounted the story, he would lean close to her and whisper words of clarification or more details. Due to the damage from his beating, Michal was not able to speak above a whisper.

What appalling suffering they had experienced. But incredibly, they both went on to speak about how grateful they were for all God had given them, how God had blessed them. They were alive and they had one another. They had faith; they would be OK. And besides, they exclaimed, "many others were far worse off than ourselves."

In the midst of a country that had been ravaged by war, without any worldly possessions, without any civil liberties and dealing with tremendous loss and suffering, Michal and his wife were free. I saw it. We all witnessed it. You could see it in their eyes. This experience caused me to look at freedom in a profoundly different way. While governments do offer one type of freedom, our greatest freedom can come only from God. It's a matter of the heart.

The *Catechism of the Catholic Church* provides tremendous insight into this topic of freedom in paragraphs 1730 through 1748, in which it states, "man is rational and therefore like God; he is created with free will and is master over his acts." [St. Iranaeus, *Adv. haeres.* 4, 4, 3:PG 7/1, 983.] (*CCC*, 1730). It is true that each person is free to act as he or she pleases, but a person is only *truly* free if his or her actions are good. To the degree that actions are bad or sinful, one actually becomes less free. The *Catechism* continues, "Human freedom is a force for growth and maturity in truth and goodness; it attains its perfection when directed toward God" (*CCC*, 1731). As a person chooses the good, the person should then experience more profound freedom. When one chooses the good and experiences this freedom, this same person becomes more the person he or she was created to be. Obviously, the converse is also true. As one makes choices opposed to God, he or she becomes less free. This is what Saint Paul meant when he wrote, "For you were called for freedom, brothers. But do not use this freedom as an opportunity for the flesh; rather, serve one another through love" (Galatians 5:13).

I suppose there is always a part of us that knows this to be true. I remember stealing a Snickers bar from the local store when I was a little boy. Yes, sad, but true. Clearly, I knew it was wrong to steal and I remember being plagued the rest of the day with guilt at what I had done. In bed that evening, I felt so bad, trapped by what I had done. I had been free to choose or not to choose to steal the candy bar, but my choosing to steal was not an appropriate use of my freedom and actually ended up causing me to experience burden and bondage. This led to other struggles such as fear of my parents finding out what I had done.

I realize this is but a simple example but it does allow us to see how an improper use of our freedom can actually cause us to be bound and in the end, cause us to be less human. Freedom is a gift given to humanity and when we use it wisely we actually become more human (which is a good thing, but I will get into that later). Sadly, when we use it for ill, when we choose against God, our freedom dehumanizes us. I have been created to be in relationship with God but when I choose to separate myself from him and attempt to live on my own, I must proceed without God and without his grace. This is, of course, a recipe for disaster.

### I See Dead People

In the movie *The Sixth Sense,* a young boy spoke a memorable line to the doctor who was caring for him. The boy stated, "I see dead people, and they don't even know they are dead." The twist to the movie was that the doctor himself was dead and he didn't even know it.

The problem, as I see it, is that most people really don't know they can be free. Or perhaps more accurately and possibly even sadder, they don't even know they are bound. This is the category into which I believe countless people fall. Almost everyone becomes so accustomed to bondage—to living in the shadows, to surviving—that most of these people are not even aware that there is another way of living.

So many individuals are bound to the troubles of their past. Countless men and women are bound to the pain and suffering caused by divorce. Others are plagued by a sense of abandonment because their fathers left home. Some are burdened by sins they committed ten, twenty or fifty years ago. These sins constantly plague their memories when they are alone and close their eyes. They are haunted.

There are situations that happened to you in the past that have left scars in you, things so personal that you swore you would never speak of them or cry about them again. Sadly, the list of examples could be almost endless. Oftentimes, these are things that you, like many others, have spent a great deal of time and energy trying to forget. You try to run away from them. "If I only run faster, farther, higher, this won't plague me anymore. I can run; I can hide; I can escape. I just have to try harder and be stronger. I can make it not hurt anymore." This simply becomes exhausting.

Other things that may bind you include fears that don't allow you to be the person you want to be. Fears don't allow you to do what you want to do. Innumerable people suffer from anger at those who have hurt or betrayed them. Others are bound by trying to conform themselves to be the person that someone else wants them to be and therefore are not fully free to be the person they should be; the type of person they are depends on whom they are with. Some are bound to things like the balances in their checking accounts, their salaries, the types of cars they drive, the size of their homes, food or a number on a bathroom scale—the list goes on and on and on.

For these people, the reality that Jesus has come so that we may have life abundantly (see John 10:10) often seems too good to be true. The voice saying *you can be free* seems too distant, too faint. They view these words as a gift offered to a select few, but certainly not to *them*. An act of grace must penetrate the hearts of such people and awaken the hope of a new way of living. This hope is deeply rooted in every human person's soul. We were created to be fully alive—to be free—and when we don't experience this, we feel a tug in our heart for something more. Our hearts cry out, "This is not what I was created for, there must be more." Bless God that it is his desire that his people live in freedom and that they experience this freedom. Thank God that it has been this way from the beginning. God desires you to be free and has always desired you to be free.

This tension is where we all live. We are free and we are also bound. The tension between living free and being bound is too often simply accepted as a necessary part of our lives. We live in degrees of freedom and bondage with a battle constantly taking place in our minds and our hearts and for our minds and our hearts. But this is not what it was like in the beginning, the very beginning. No, in the very beginning there was total freedom.

*Love will relationship w/ the Way, Truth & Life*

## JOURNEY TO GOD'S HEART

*Listening:*
John 10:7–11

*Reflecting:*

*attentive.*

To you, what does it mean to be *free*?
How do you experience the abundant life
of which Jesus spoke?

*Conversing:*
"Dear God, what I want most from you is…"
"Jesus, what causes me fear is…"

## CHAPTER TWO

## FREEDOM FIRST

"I LOVE YOU, UNCLE DAVE." IT WAS THE FIRST TIME I HAD HEARD those words. My heart melted. I remember it like it was yesterday. I was reaching into the back seat of my older brother's car, buckling my niece's car seat. Our eyes met and she blurted out, "I love you, Uncle Dave."

I was home on vacation, and my niece was just beginning to talk. Due to the fact that I had been away at school, I had not been around her much, so she really didn't know me well, which made me that much more susceptible when I heard those sweet words. I was putty in the hands of a two-year-old, hers for the taking. My heart simply melted. At that moment I would have given my niece anything. What sweet words!

First words are important. Who can forget the famous words spoken from the first man to set foot on the moon? "One giant step..."

I can still remember the first homily I gave as a deacon. I had spoken in front of people too many times to remember, but this was different. This was a homily, and it was my first homily.

Finally, I was being let loose on the People of God; Lord save them.

What would I say?

How would I say it?

What kind of media turnout would there be?

I remember practicing in the chapel late in the day with only the flickering of the candles and the light of a street lamp slipping through the stained-glass windows. All alone, I prepared for the homily that would enlighten an entire congregation, maybe even a generation. It was quite possible that the world as we knew it would never be the same....

I don't remember much about people's response to that homily, but still now, many years later, I remember that it had to do with popcorn, salt and Christians bringing flavor to the world. So much for enlightenment and changing the world, but it was my first homily and I still remember giving it. I don't remember my third, my tenth or my one-hundredth homily, but I do remember the first.

Firsts are important. So in the first chapter of the first book of the Bible we read that God created man and blessed him (see Genesis 1:28). The first thing God did was not to instruct, teach, command or rebuke us. Instead, he blesses us. God, who had the freedom to create or not create, created humanity in love and bestowed his blessing on us. Then he encouraged men and women to be fruitful and multiply; he invited human beings to share in his amazing gift of creation. He was also blessing and encouraging people to be wholly who they had been created to be, and that includes being *free*.

In Sirach 15:14–15 we read, "When God, in the beginning, created man, / he made him subject to his own free choice. / If you choose you can keep the commandments." We have the freedom to choose; it is up to us.

This same message can be seen in the second chapter in Genesis in the second creation account. God created Adam and Eve and told them: "You are free to eat from any of the trees of the garden except the tree of knowledge of good and bad. From that tree you shall not eat; the moment you eat from it you are surely doomed to die" (Genesis 2:16–17).

This is significant. We have been blessed by God and have been given the freedom to choose him and his blessing—or to choose something else. God, being perfectly and totally free, breathed life into the human family and created us free to be free. I believe that the whole of creation and salvation history, our very existence, is predicated on this fundamental reality that we have been blessed and we are free.

God did not have to create us free. He could have created little puppets that were totally controlled by him. But as Sirach and the *Catechism* (*CCC*, 1730) state, each person was created free and is the master of his or her own acts.

Cardinal Christoph Schönborn of Vienna, Austria, explains this very well. He said, "God creates in absolute freedom, nothing forces him to.... This has immense consequences for our understanding of our world and ourselves.... He has given creatures real independence.... God has created freedom, which is the greater marvel of all in creation." The cardinal goes on to say, "it is because we are created in God in complete freedom that we can really be ourselves."[1]

*Trouble in Paradise*

But where did things go wrong? If we are all free, and free to be ourselves, where did things go so terribly wrong? Let's once again look at the world of Adam and Eve. Their world was free of chaos, suffering and pain. They took evening strolls, hand-in-hand, through a land flowing with milk and honey. Adam and Eve were freely walking naked in the midst of the Garden, with God. (Naked! Now, maybe that is a little too free.) It was a different time. The world was as it should be.

As Adam and Eve were created free, they could choose either to obey God's invitation or not. Adam and Eve, you and I (especially I), have the choice, and all too often we opt for something other than freedom, something other than love, something other than God. Adam and Eve's decision was simply whether or not to eat the fruit. The choice was up to them. It was simple and clear. But the Serpent confused things. "Did he really say...?" The Serpent has a way of twisting very simple, clear things, which makes us begin to question what deep down inside we know to be true.

This conversation has taken place between child and parent from the beginning of time: "I would like you to be home by 11:00 PM sharp."

As the night progresses and the dreaded hour is getting close, your friend asks if you *have* to be in by eleven o'clock. "What exactly did your mom say?"

"Well, she said that she wanted me in by eleven o'clock."

"Aha, I see. So she didn't *really* say that you *had* to be in by eleven o'clock; she merely said she would *like* you to be in by eleven o'clock." A budding lawyer, no doubt. But we all get the point.

Adam and Eve were free to act, free to choose. It was not simply whether to have an apple or not. There were plenty of apples in the Garden. It was a choice for this specific apple from this specific tree, or better yet, a choice to obey or not. It is so often merely a choice. "I have set before you life and death, the blessing and the curse. Choose life...." (Deuteronomy 30:19).

Which of us has never felt that tug? Who hasn't waged this battle in the depths of our hearts? "I want it. I want that one. I want it now." As Adam and Eve did, we also many times choose the curse. We choose chains and shackles instead of freedom. Now, due to original sin (and lots of not-so-original sin), man is no longer free. The consequences were dramatic, immediate and lasting. Thankfully, however, they are not permanent.

Man, who was at one moment free, was now consumed with fear and full of shame. Adam and Eve, who were once free to walk in the Garden as they were, were no longer comfortable with their bodies and they had to cover themselves. (They really were free when they were naked.) Sadly, Adam and Eve began to hide from God. How tragic.

Now God had to go looking for Adam. "Where are you?" (Genesis 3:9). Three more words, but what different words from the first three, "You are free." God had to go looking for them, and he has had to go looking for us. We who should constantly be sitting at his feet, waiting on him, laughing with him, have hidden ourselves from the one who loves us. Amazingly, he plays the game and comes looking. "Where are you? Marco? Polo? Ready or not..." How childish, really. Hiding from God as if he does not know where we are every moment of every day. But we are free, and he comes looking.

One of the reasons that Adam and Eve hid from God was that they were no longer comfortable with how God created them. In the Garden they were free to be themselves. After the Fall, this was no longer the case. They no longer loved themselves. To be as they were created was no longer good enough.

*Free to Be Me*
What a gift of God it is for you to be free to be yourself. I am aware that for some of you, this does not seem like much of a gift. If you don't like yourself, then the idea of being able to be yourself is not that attractive. Some people would rather be anyone else more than who they are. But, and hear this well, you were created to like, even to love, yourself. This is not strange, conceited or weird. We all need to be able to stand in front of a mirror and say, "I love you." I know, I know, it sounds so weird and corny, but it really is important. If you can't love yourself, how can you really love anyone else or allow others to love you? You have been created in the image and likeness of a holy, living God. This gives you value and worth

beyond all telling. When you experience this, you experience freedom.

I am reminded of a Calvin and Hobbes cartoon. I am a huge Calvin fan, I think because I can so often see myself in him. In this one particular cartoon Calvin is standing in front of a full-length mirror wearing only his tighty-whities, flexing his little, scrawny muscles and saying, "Made in God's own image, yes-sir-ee." Hobbes, who is tolerating the show, smartly counters, "God must have a goofy sense of humor."

I love it. Calvin, in all of his glory, is appreciating God's creation, himself. And so it is with you. God looks at you standing in front of that mirror and loves what *you* see. God appreciates it, God marvels at it, God delights in it. How can you not delight in it too? You are wonderfully made.

I am not saying I don't have parts of me I don't like or things that I see that I wish were different. I hate it that sometimes I am more concerned about me than about others. I can't stand it that I am thoughtless and fail to do the simplest things that would brighten someone's day. It bugs me to no end that sometimes rather than getting up early to pray, I roll over and go back to sleep. Or that at times my pride does not allow me to love the way I know God wants me to. These things drive me crazy, but they are not me. I don't define myself by my weakness or my sin; rather, I let God define who I am.

I am a child of an eternal God who is wild about me. It is imperative for us to remember that, first and foremost, you and I are children of a loving Father and that we happen to make mistakes; we sin. We are not first sinners who happen to be children of God. We must define ourselves in the positive—who we are, children—not in the negative by what we do, sin. Sin must never define you. This is really important. God loves me, not because of what I do, not because I am a priest, but because I am *his*. I am his creation, and, as the psalmist writes, he keeps me as the apple of his eye (see Psalm 17:8).

It is not simply that God loves me, but that I am lovable and so are you. In my experience, most of the people who question God's love, when really pushed, can admit that they believe that God is love, but they have to say that they do not believe that they personally are lovable. They do not see their value and dignity and therefore are not able to see themselves as good. "Father Dave, how could God love me? You don't know what I have done." Honestly, that doesn't matter. God *is* love (see 1 John 4:8) and he can do nothing *but* love. God does not make a choice to love; rather, love is his nature. I don't wake up in the morning and decide to be human, I just am.

We need to be able to ask God for the grace to see ourselves as he sees us. This is one of the foundations for our ability to grow in freedom. The part of you that you don't like is holding you captive. There is such great freedom in being you. You don't have to be someone else, and you don't have to be who you think people want you to be. Just be you. The minute that you are able to see your personal beauty and value and stop trying to be someone or something else is such a freeing moment. At that moment you can stop surviving and start living.

This is not some feel-good, self-help, tell-myself-something-long-enough-and-I'll-believe-it mantra. It is a fundamental truth of our faith. You are created good. It has been such a blessing for me to be able to pray with people when they come to understand that they are fundamentally good. They are not a mistake or an accident but are a son or daughter of a God who passionately loves them. I remember one young woman who had gone through terrible struggles. She had lost her mother at a young age and had made choices that were very destructive. She had done things that she regretted and she really had doubts about a God that loved, not to mention doubting that she herself was actually lovable.

Jennifer and I met many times over several months, talking about her experience and her frustration with God. I invited her to be honest with God and to share her frustration and anger with him. I told her that he was a big boy and that he could take it. She did not have to hide her feelings from God and she could freely share them with him. And anyway, it wasn't as if God did not know what she was thinking or feeling. I told her that God was deeply in love with her no matter what.

One time, she had been nervously playing with a penny she had found on the floor of my office during our meeting. A few days later, I received a letter from her. She wrote:

> I was thinking about the penny that I was playing with the whole time we were talking. Pennies go through a lot of "stuff" too. They get passed from person to person and

dropped in the mud and stepped on but no matter how dirty and beaten up they get, their worth stays the same. You know some pennies have an easy life because they are all shiny but then you get the black ones and you know they've been through a lot. It's just like people. Some of us are shiny and some of us are dirty and beat up, but we are all of equal worth and we are all loved. I feel like I'm one of those dirty pennies in the gutter, but you picked me up, brushed me off and showed me that I have worth. You told me a lot about a God who loves me and doesn't want me to hurt or hate or be angry. For the first time I'm starting to think that maybe that could be true.

It is true, Jennifer, and you have expressed this far better than I ever could. We do have a God who is deeply in love with us. As I said earlier, God does not make a decision to love. Rather, he simply loves; it is his nature and he can never act against this nature. God cannot love in degrees. He cannot love more and he cannot love less; all he can do is love. It doesn't matter how much one has grown in the spiritual life, this is a reality that one never "outgrows." It is fundamental to all we believe.

I remember one time in seminary when I was going through a particularly difficult period. In the matter of a few months, I had lost a close friend to death as well as my four-month-old goddaughter Rebecca. Everything in my life was barren and confused. I attended Mass daily but felt like a spectator rather than a participant. My personal prayer was dry with no sense of any real consolation. I remember writing in my journal, "Oh God, you seem like a stranger I once knew." It was probably the most difficult time in my formation as a priest.

One evening I was in the chapel praying—whining, actually. "God, do you care? Are you there? Do you hear me?" I recall so clearly God breaking in and that moment telling me that he loved me. I was taken aback, since it had been some time since I had really been able to hear God. "Well, it is nice to hear from you. But the issue is not your loving me. It is about pain, and death and darkness." Once again, I heard God tell me that he loved me. I sat in that small chapel and wept. He was right (there, I said it). It *was* about his love for me. In the midst of everything, God had not abandoned me. He was there and he loved me.

A few weeks after this experience I remember having lunch with a fellow seminarian. We were sharing about what God was doing in our lives. "I am really coming to understand God's love for me in a more profound way," I said.

John looked at me with kind of a quizzical look. "Um, Dave, you are going to be ordained in two years. You should probably know that. That's pretty much first-grade CCD material."

And of course I did know that before, but God was revealing his love to me in a new and more profound way. It still happens. God is always bringing me back to his love. I now understand this love more than I did ten years ago and hopefully ten years from now I will understand it more than I do today.

When we discover this love, we experience a deep freedom. God is love; I am lovable. This freedom is God's gift flowing from his deep love for us and I believe it is one of the first steps we take on the road to greater freedom. God desires us to live in his love and to live freely. This is as it was in the beginning. God passionately loved his creation and he created us so that we could be free to love him and be loved by him.

So it can be said that this is the rest of the story, the rest of salvation history: a love story of God searching for his people. The Creator is searching while the created ones hide, fearful of what God wants and afraid of what he will say or do. Of course the created ones are yet unaware that their God will run to them. So they hide, not knowing that God simply wants to find them so that they may be free once again.

### Being Found by God

It is possible to be free. You really can be free. I have prayed and talked with thousands of people and when I talk about freedom something in them clicks. "I can be free? I don't have to be bound? I don't have to be afraid? I don't have to hide anymore?" For some, it simply sounds too good to be true. But something deep inside of them knows it to be true. It just has to be. As I've been saying, it is how we were created.

Sadly, of course, too many people have become accustomed to being bound, to being chained. It is amazing to what we can become accustomed. Once I went to the doctor because I was having some problems with my voice.

(Apparently, I talk too much. Who knew?) The doctor and I had been talking for a while when she asked me if I were hoarse. I replied I wasn't, that actually my voice felt quite strong lately. She then stated, "Yes, you are. Your voice is very hoarse; it's 'fried' and damaged."

I was a little taken aback.

"You see, Father, you have gotten used to it being this way. Your voice has been damaged for so long, you simply don't recognize it anymore. But I can tell." So she had me do some voice exercises and I could hear it. She was right. I had simply become accustomed to hearing my voice this way and couldn't recall it being different.

The same is true for many people. You may be so used to being bound that you don't even recognize bondage. People can live with so much pain or fear that they simply get used to it. As one young lady wrote me, "Father, I got used to the pain and the hurt. I became numb!" So many people stop dreaming and hoping and laughing. They don't even realize there is a different way to live. In fact, they really aren't living anymore; they are, rather, simply surviving.

But, when God breaks into the human heart, and whispers to his people that they are free, something so deep within them, deeper than anything they have ever listened to before, tells them it is OK to believe. At that moment, the person begins the journey back to life. This journey will lead them to the very heart of God, a place of freedom.

For some, you hear these words and immediately think, "Not I. I have struggled too long. I am in too deep. The sin is too great. The hurt is too powerful. The addiction is too strong. The shame is too overwhelming. Freedom is not possible for me." But I'm here to tell you that that is a lie. You *can* be free. It is how you were created and what you are created for. Search your heart; look deeper. You know it is true.

For others, you hear this invitation to freedom and it stirs your heart. You know instantly what it is that you want to be freed from. You are not sure exactly what freedom looks like and you're not totally sure what binds you and you certainly have no idea how you are going to get there, but you know almost instinctively that you are not currently living the freedom that God intended. You just know that when Jesus said he came so that we may have life abundantly, you are not living what he had in mind. Your heart tells you there must be more. There has to be more, and there is.

In the end, it doesn't make a huge difference where you are when you hear God's call to freedom. God is a God of freedom and he wants all of his people to be free. No matter where you are on your journey of faith, God wants you to be freer. There is always more freedom: more grace, more forgiveness, more mercy, more God. I know that God wants me to be freer today than yesterday. This is why I seek more of God daily.

Freedom is a reality. It is how we were created. Freedom is something we need to get back to. It is not something that we have to create or develop. It is. We are free already; we just need to claim it. The goal of freedom is not becoming, rather it is being. We need to let God show us the things that bind us and then let him set us free. The challenge is getting rid of the things that hinder us from being free.

In order to grow deeper in freedom, you must make a decision that you want to be free. It may seem obvious that if someone is bound, then that person must want to be free, but this is not always the case. Sometimes bondage seems preferable because it is more familiar, and people know that the path to freedom may be difficult. But it is the only path that leads to life. Are you willing to begin to tread down that path? As is so often the case, the choice is yours. If you choose to walk on this path, God will lead you along until you know for sure that freedom is ahead.

## JOURNEY TO GOD'S HEART

*Listening:*
Psalm 139

*Reflecting:*
How and where do you hide from God?
Can you stand in front of a mirror and
say to yourself, "I love you"?

*Conversing:*
"Jesus, I want to be free because..."
"Dear God, I know you love me because..."

<br>

## CHAPTER THREE

## FREEDOM FROM

FROM THE BEGINNING, GOD INTENDED US TO BE FREE. BUT WITH the cunning work of the Serpent and the cooperation of Adam and Eve, human beings fell from grace. From that very moment, God was already putting into place a plan to make his people free again. "I will put enmity between you and the woman, / and between your offspring and hers; / He will strike at your head, / while you strike at his heel" (Genesis 3:15). In many ways, salvation history is a story of God working his plan in order to free his people. (As it has been said: "I love it when a plan comes together.") God wanted his people free and he still does, and he will do whatever it takes to free them. In some cases, it means using an unlikely candidate, such as a person who can't speak very well and who is full of questions. One such person would be none other than Moses.

I love Moses, and I love taking my nieces and nephews to the movies. When those two things come together, we have a real party. For me, everything about taking my nieces and nephews to the movies is fun. Children get so excited and they aren't afraid to show it. Somewhere along the line, we grow up and forget what it is to have the excitement and anticipation of a child. Movies with nieces and nephews remind me that it is OK to be giddy with excitement. The popcorn, candy and pop—it's all just too exciting. When they are with Uncle Dave, they get lots of everything. And the great thing about *being* Uncle Dave is that at the end of the movie, I take them home and leave them with their mom and dad, who get to deal with the sugar rush. Oh, celibate life really does have its moments.

I took my nieces and nephews to the movie *Prince of Egypt,* an animated film that tells the story of Moses. At one scene in the movie when Moses was walking in the desert, I said to my niece, who was sitting on my lap, "Now pay attention, pretty soon he is going to run into a bush that is on fire and the bush is going to talk to him." Beth turned to me and said, "Have you seen this movie?" I assured her that I had not.

I must admit I was a little bothered that my four-year-old niece was not impressed with my knowledge of Scripture, but I was able to enjoy the movie nonetheless. Sure enough, Moses did encounter God in the burning bush. When it happened, my niece turned once again and said quite emphatically, "You've seen this." Not until we got home and I showed her in the Bible the story of the burning bush would she believe that I had not already seen the movie. It's tough to impress kids these days.

Whether I'm reading it in the Bible or watching it on the big screen, I love the scene of Moses and the burning bush. (You can read about it in Exodus 3—4.) Moses was out for his daily stroll and an angel of the Lord appeared to him in a burning bush:

> As he looked on, he was surprised to see that the bush, though on fire, was not consumed. So Moses decided, "I must go over to look at this remarkable sight, and see why the bush is not burned." (Exodus 3:2–3)

How calm and cool is Moses? His tranquil, collected response is much different from what mine would have been. Think about it, a flaming bush that ends up talking to you. Come on, I probably would have acted like I didn't even see it and run away. But not Moses. Nope, he is one cool customer: "I must go look at this remarkable sight."

God then says to Moses:

> I have witnessed the affliction of my people in Egypt and have heard their cry of complaint against their slave drivers, so I know well what they are suffering. Therefore I have come down to *rescue* [the Hebrew root word means "to be freed" or "to be brought out"] them from the hands of the Egyptians and lead them out of that land into a good and spacious land, a land flowing with milk and honey. (Exodus 3:7–8, emphasis mine)

In other words, "I want my people free, and you, Moses, are going to help them get there."

This is so important. We wonder, "does God even hear me; does he care; does he see my situation or feel my sorrow?" Often we feel that we pour out our hearts to a God who may or may not be there. But God lets Moses know that he is there.

"I have witnessed the affliction.... I have heard their cry...." God has never, nor will he ever, close his eyes or ears to us. The people of Israel were in bondage and they were suffering. They wondered if God noticed. He had, and it was time for him to act. God had chosen Moses as his representative and he was going to lead them to freedom. He would lead his people to "a good and spacious land, a land flowing with milk and honey" (Exodus 3:8). Moses was to be "The Man"—if only he could believe it.

Moses is clearly a little apprehensive about all of this. He really doesn't quite get it at first. This cluelessness seems to be a pretty common trait for many of the people God chooses to use. I actually find great relief in that. Thank God he is patient with us.

It is important to look at what God said to Moses in order to understand how he is going to set his people free:

> Say to the Israelites: I am the LORD. I will free you from the forced labor of the Egyptians and will deliver you from their slavery. I will rescue you by my outstretched arm and with mighty acts of judgment. I will take you as my own people, and you shall have me as your God. You will know that I, the LORD, am your God when I free you from the labor of the Egyptians and bring you into the land which I swore to give to Abraham, Isaac and Jacob. I will give it to you as your own possession—I, the LORD! (Exodus 6:6–8)

This passage is key because it reveals some fundamental points about what it means for us to be free. First, Moses doubted that the people could be free, as if their freedom was up to him. It was not. Freedom is an act of God. God frees us, not Moses. God said to Moses, "I will free you.... I will deliver you.... I will take you as my own.... And you will know that I am God when I free you."

How amazing is that? This really is God's work. God did not tell Moses that it was his responsibility to free them. Rather, it is God who is going to do the freeing. This should come as a great relief to anyone who wants to be free or wants to see others free. Freedom is about God's work in our hearts. It has much more to do with his power, grace and love than it does with our ability to will something. I can long to see someone free and pray with him or her for that freedom, but ultimately, it is God's work that brings freedom.

The amazing thing is that once a person comes to know this freedom, he or she will also come to know God. "You will know that I am God when I free you." How unbelievably beautiful! There is a direct relationship between our being free and our coming to know that the Lord is God.

*I Am the God of Freedom*

It is a very difficult thing for those who are experiencing great bondage to know God. There is something fundamental about the human heart in that it was created to be free, and if that freedom is hindered it becomes a stumbling block to our ability to know God. In this account, God clearly says that when you experience freedom, true freedom, which can only come from him, this will lead you to an understanding of who God is. It is as if God is saying, "I am the God of Freedom. If you know and experience freedom, you will know and experience me."

Sadly, Moses doubted that this freedom was possible. He wasn't the only one who doubted; the people themselves doubted they could be free. "[W]hen Moses told this to the Israelites, they would not listen to him because of their dejection and hard slavery" (Exodus 6:9).

Should we expect anything different from them? For goodness' sake, they were *slaves*. Slavery was their life. They were forced to labor and build and they lived with shackles around their ankles. It's who they were. It was how they identified themselves and it was how they defined themselves. Their entire world had become chains, forced labor and masters. This was their existence and they were so bound to it they could not see anything else. They had learned to define themselves by their bondage. "Who is this Moses guy anyway, speaking of freedom? Is he blind to our situation?"

Bondage strips us of our human dignity. We are no longer people, no longer sons and daughters, we are slaves or addicts or sinners or adulterers or liars or fat or ugly or worthless or fearful or, or, or... We get so used to our bondage that we begin to define ourselves by it. "I am a slave. We are all slaves." This becomes our world—a world in which we believe there is no way out. We begin to believe the lies, which only perpetuate our bondage.

The people were not able to hear Moses. It was simply more than they could imagine. Moses returned to God, rather dejected, I would think, and he informed God that the people really were not that interested in being free. "A good idea, God, but it doesn't look like they are going to cooperate. Can I go now?"

What God does next is so important and so profound. Of course they were not going to cooperate; they saw themselves only as slaves; they could not cooperate. They were not free enough to say, "Oh, yes Moses, we'll go with you." They were slaves. God knew this, so again he sent Moses on a journey to deliver a message, but this time not to the Israelites. He sent Moses to speak to the one who was binding them, the pharaoh. God knew that if the people were going to be free, then Moses was going to have to speak to the source of their bondage. Moses could tell the people that they are free until the cows came home, but if he never dealt with the source of their slavery, the people would never be free.

This is true in our lives as well. I can tell you that you are free. I can explain that God created you to be free. I can furnish you with plenty of examples. While this may stir something in your heart, you will not be free until you allow God to address the "pharaoh" in your life. I know that this can be a scary thing. It was scary for Moses and he had a hard time believing that it would do any good. His reasoning seemed to make sense. If the people are not going to listen to him, surely Pharaoh is not going to listen. "And besides, I don't talk so good." Poor Moses, you've got to love him; he still thinks it's all about him.

You see, Moses still thinks God was asking *him* to free the people. Clearly, he did not pay close attention to what God had said to him. "I am the Lord. I will free you." It is essential that we understand this point if we are going to be free. It is God who reveals to us our bondage; he reveals our pharaoh, and he will set us free. This is also very helpful for anyone whom God has called to lead others to freedom. It is God who initiates the process that will ultimately lead us to freedom. God leads us to the Promised Land, and it is by his hand that we will be free to go. "I will free you.... I will rescue you.... I will take you." Freedom has much more to do with God than it does with you. It is God's action in your life that will bring you freedom. You simply need to cooperate. While it is easy to say this, it can be very, very difficult to do it. Don't believe anyone who tells you this road is going to be easy. It is not. But it is possible.

The sad reality is that many people are so bound that they cannot imagine themselves being free and because of this, they never begin to travel the road to freedom. I have met far too many people like this. They are so bound, so caught up in their fear, that they are not willing or able to let God bring them to freedom. This is sad, because he is continually stretching out his hand in order to lead us to his freedom. (See Exodus 7:5 and Psalm 18:17.)

*Confrontation Time*
Mary wondered if she could ever be free. You see Mary had been struggling with an eating disorder for nearly ten years. What a devious and destructive bondage this is. Just as in the case with Moses, when I began to talk to Mary and told her that she could be free she could only look at me with a blank stare. She didn't know how this was possible nor did she know what freedom could look like. "I can't imagine what it would be like to be free," she would tell me. "The thought of it actually frightens me."

Sounds kind of strange, doesn't it? Fear of freedom. But it is a real thing and, as I now know, this fear is actually very common. Simply the thought of life without chains causes people to be afraid. They have become so accustomed to their slavery that they are not certain they can live without it.

It's not such an easy thing to ask for freedom. I have prayed with many people who were aware of what their bondage was, but they were not able to ask for freedom. Mary would say to me, "I can't imagine what life without an eating disorder would be like." She described her disorder like a cloud that is always hanging over her. She didn't necessarily like the fact that it was there, but it was always there. It was her constant companion and, as odd as it may sound, she found comfort in this. In a very strange way, the bondage was dependable; she could count on it.

Mary had become used to being bound and she actually thought it was a safe place. The truth is that the thought of freedom really can be scary. When someone has never really lived free, to invite that person to a life of freedom is like asking him or her to go to a foreign land, a place very unfamiliar. Freedom may mean a whole new way of thinking, a new way of living, a new way of relating. People prefer to stay in bondage. At least they are used to it.

People like Mary who have eating disorders have all kinds of rules about their eating. There is food that is safe and food that is unsafe. They may have rules about when they can and cannot eat. Oftentimes they refuse dates for fear of having to eat something, and they don't attend parties because there is going to be food there and everyone will want them to eat or will watch them eat. Some have lived this way for so long they can't imagine what it would be like to live differently.

"Father Dave, to be honest, I don't even know what food I like. My eating has been controlled for so long, I don't even remember." The thought of eating whatever she wanted was so foreign to her she simply could not imagine it. I only use eating disorders as an example. It could be drugs, pornography, fear, anger, hatred. For a person such as Mary, the thought of living free causes anxiety.

"Really, Father Dave, I don't know what I would do. It [the cloud] has always been there. I can't imagine being without it." I would ask her, "Do you want it to be gone? Do you want to be free of it?"

"I just don't know. I don't know if I can do it."

I would encourage Mary to think about what it would be like to be free. I have found this to be a good exercise that helps the person to dream about what a life of freedom may look like. It helps them see that there may be another way of living. What will the land flowing with milk and honey look like?

"I think a lot about my wedding day," she would say. "What am I going to do at the reception? On my wedding day, I want to be able to eat my wedding cake and not freak out. That would be great."

Mary and I would often meet and pray. We started with the first step, praying for a heart that wants to be free. I remember one evening when we were talking and she looked at me, with a little fear and trepidation (actually a lot of fear) and said, "Father Dave, I think I am ready." She did not have to say anything more. I knew what she meant; she was ready to ask God to set her free. So she made a very simple prayer. "Jesus, I would like to want to be free." It was a beginning.

Step by step Mary continued to seek God's freedom. She continued to give her fears and anxieties to the Lord. We continued to pray. Over time, Mary came to a place where she really and truly longed to be free.

I remember the evening she prayed to be free. Mary prayed against the disorder and asked God to free her from it. She spoke to the disorder as if it were a person and told it to leave. She said that she did not want to live in its bondage anymore. She said she was a daughter of God, not a girl with an eating disorder. She proclaimed that she was created to be and to live free. "Be gone, in Jesus' name, be gone." Two simple words, repeated, yet they were terribly difficult to utter. Mary had begun the path to freedom. It would not be an easy road, but she was on the road to freedom. She was beginning to live again.

I also remember her wedding day. It was about the time for the cake to be cut and several of her friends came running up to me, saying, "Father Dave, Mary said you have to come quick. It is time to cut the cake." I was in the middle of a conversation with some people and they were somewhat surprised that I had to attend the cutting of the cake. "Does the priest usually have something to do with this custom?" they asked. I watched the simple ceremony with tears in my eyes. Mary was beaming as her husband's hand gently helped her slice the cake. There was a sparkle in her eyes at the moment of indecision as her husband contemplated whether or not to generously spread the frosting across her face. I would guess that for most brides the traditional cutting and eating of the wedding cake is not the major event of her wedding day, but for Mary it was. It was one sign of her freedom.

I would like to say that Mary never had another moment's struggle with her disorder, but that is not the case. There are rare times that are difficult for her. But she has tasted freedom, literally, and is experiencing so much more of it. She strives to keep moving forward, and she finds God walking on the journey with her more than ever before. This continues to give her comfort. We should not be surprised that the journey is difficult and at times lengthy. Going back to Moses, we remember that the journey to the Promised Land took quite some time. Do not lose sight of this. The point is that it is better to be on the path of freedom and experience difficulties than to remain a slave in the land of the pharaoh in your life.

*Living on the Edge*
When I was first learning to ride a bike, I started out learning to ride in our large yard, where if I fell, I would fall on grass and not get hurt. After being taught to ride in the relative safety of the yard, one day it was decided that I was ready to ride in the neighborhood. (By whom, I can't recall, but I think my older brother had something to do with it.) I have to admit I was both excited and apprehensive. What if I wreck? I'm not going to be falling on grass this time. Am I going to fall? What will it be like? Am I ready? All good questions, but eventually I knew I had to

begin to ride my bike away from our yard. So there I was, on the top of a small hill. My brother gave me a little push. Down I went, smack into the back of our neighbor's car. (Thanks for the help, Jim.) But I got up, dusted myself off and tried again. Soon I was riding all over the neighborhood with the other boys. I was free. Now I could go anywhere. Well, at least I could now ride my bike to the Circle K.

It was scary to leave the confines of my family's yard but there was more out there that I needed to see. Freedom is living "out there," which can be difficult. It may mean living without the walls that have protected you for so long. While it is true that you may believe that those walls protect and keep you safe, oftentimes they have become the place of your bondage. They don't allow you to live in the light; they keep you in shadows. This is not living; it is surviving; it is hiding. Your walls must come down.

The journey to freedom is filled with tremendous moments of grace but, as I have stated, it is also difficult. We can't forget that the same people who were singing God's praises after they had crossed through the Red Sea ("We're free! We're free!") are the same people who cursed God and Moses:

> But with their patience worn out by the journey, the people complained against God and Moses, "Why have you brought us up from Egypt to die in this desert, where there is no food or water? We are disgusted with this wretched food!"(Numbers 21:4–5)

Imagine. God had done the impossible. He had led the people out of slavery, kept them alive with bread from heaven—and now they "have grown impatient with God and are disgusted with this wretched food"? How quickly they forgot. "We were better off as slaves!" they protested. How that must have broken the heart of God. But, sadly, this is altogether too common an experience. At times men and women will begin down the path of freedom only to quit because it becomes too hard. "I was better off a slave." Too many times to remember, I have had people say to me, "I thought I was free, I thought I was over this. If I had known it was going to be so difficult, I would never have begun." They felt as if they had been duped. "Sure you led us out of slavery only to let us die here in the desert." But the truth is that God did not let them die and he continued to lead them. Our journey, too, is perilous, but it is one we must take if we are going to be free.

Finally, if one is to be truly free, you must pray for a heart of gratitude and the grace to remember. The Israelite people forgot too soon what God had led them from. Their sin was one of forgetfulness and ingratitude. We must pray that we never forget the slavery God has led us out of. We must keep our eyes fixed on the hand of God that has led us to this place and will continue to lead us to the Promised Land. Will it take forty years for you? Probably not. But even if it does, there is grace in the journey and God will reveal himself along the way. You are not walking alone. If it takes forty years, forty days or forty minutes, it doesn't really matter. What matters most is that at the end of the journey, another one of

God's chosen ones has come into the freedom of the Promised Land.

JOURNEY TO GOD'S HEART

*Listening:*
Psalm 118:1–9

*Reflecting:*
What would it look like for you to be free?
What is your pharaoh?

*Conversing:*
"I am beginning to see my slavery, Lord..."
"Lord, make me want to want freedom..."

## CHAPTER FOUR

## FREEDOM GONE

HAVE YOU EVER BEEN GUILTY OF SOMETHING? I MEAN REALLY guilty? Caught red-handed, no-way-out guilty? It was the night of the senior keg party and I was a sophomore in high school. It was *the* major party at the end of the year and Bob (a friend of mine) and I had been invited to attend. For a lowly sophomore, it was a pretty big event.

Now, to be honest, I really did not lie to my parents that often—stretched the truth, sometimes, sure. But outright lying was really rare. However, I had been invited to go to the *senior* beer bash. I just had to go. So I stood in front of my mother, and when she asked if I was going to go to the party, responded, "What party? Oh, that one. Nope, not me, only a sophomore, you know," as I marched out of the house, heading to the party.

To this day, I am not sure how my mom knew. She just did. Moms just know. I think it has something to do with the womb. At any rate, my sister showed up at the party and told me that Mom knew I was there and she wanted me to come home.

"What do you mean she knows? If you don't tell her that I am here she won't know." I tried to draw my sister into my web.

"Dave, she knows. Get home." This was not going to turn out well.

I still remember the sight. My mom was sitting up in her bed in the soft, dim light with a rosary in her hand. It was magical; the gentle light actually caused her tears to glisten on her cheeks. How *do* moms do it?

"I'm sorry, Mom."

"I am disappointed in you."

Oh, come on; fight fair, anything but that. Clearly, she was going to play by her own set of rules. It was obvious that the only just and virtuous thing for her to do would be to yell and ground me until I had my own children. But no, she had pulled the "I'm disappointed in you" card.

I had nothing. I was guilty. I headed back to my room to prepare for what I knew would be a long sentence, when my mom asked me where I was going. I stated that I was heading to my cell. She then amazed me again. "I thought I told you that you could spend the night at Bob's house."

"Well, I kind of thought I blew that."

"I told you that you could go. We will deal with this later." You have got to be kidding me. Must you throw salt into the wound? So I joined my friends at Bob's house for what proved to be a pretty miserable evening. Guilt has a way of spoiling a night with friends. I felt bad that I had lied to my mom and there was no way I was could enjoy myself. I found myself wanting to go home and tell her that I was really, really sorry. Oddly, I wanted to get my punishment underway. I knew I had done something wrong and I wanted things to be right. I began thinking of what I could do to make it right, what could I do to show her I really was sorry. That night, I broke my mom's heart and she, in return, taught me about mercy.

## Nothing Personal

As a people, we are guilty. It is easy for us to blame our guilt on Adam and Eve. We really don't want to take responsibility for it. In that regard, we are no different from Adam. When God asked him why he ate the fruit, he stated, "Eve gave it to me—not my fault." What a weasel. Anyway, we all probably need to hear the words of Jesus, "Let the one among you who is without sin be the first to throw a stone" (John 8:7).

All of us have "sinned and are deprived of the glory of God" (Romans 3:23). In order for us to understand the freedom that has been won for us, it is important that we come to fully understand our guilt. If we are to be free, then we need to be able to recognize our sin first.

We don't really talk a lot about sin. I mean, when was the last time you heard a great homily on sin? I think some priests are a little anxious about speaking on sin because they are so often aware of their own sin and feel slightly hypocritical speaking on the topic. This is unfortunate, because in general we do better when we speak on a subject we know a lot about, and sin definitely would be one of those subjects.

One time my family came from Arizona to visit me in Ohio. My nephew, who was about six at the time, asked me what happens in Ohio if you get pulled over by the police. I was not sure what he meant and he explained that in Arizona you get a ticket. I explained that this was the case in Ohio as well. He told me that I should speed up so that I would get a ticket. I was a little confused and informed him that I did not want a ticket. To which he responded, "But Uncle Dave, you are going to need a ticket to get on the plane to come home with us." Cute, huh? I went on to clarify for him that there was a difference in the two types of tickets and that I would not want to get a speeding ticket. He then gazed at me with a sad, pathetic look on his face and said, "Uncle Dave, it was a joke." Right.

In some ways, I think we view sin a lot like getting a speeding ticket. We speed, get a ticket, pay the fine and move on. There is nothing personal about it. We broke a law; we receive our punishment. It is settled. There is not much personal investment on either my side or the police officer's side. I have never yet met an officer who took my speeding personally. (Obviously, this is all hypothetical in the attempt to illustrate a point.) A police officer has never come up to my car window with tears in his eyes, offended that I had not yielded the right of way. I am not sure what I would say if an officer pulled me over to say how I had hurt his feelings by not obeying the traffic signal.

The opposite is also true. I have never found myself crying as I got pulled over. (That is not to say that some of you are not above this, if you think it may get you out of a ticket. You know who you are.) It's not the way it works. Tickets are a simple, clean, almost sterile transaction between the enforcer of the law and the offender.

Sin is not like that at all. However, I think we often make it out to be that way. We sin, get caught or turn ourselves in, get our ticket or penance, pay it or pray it and move on. We make it out as a nice, clean transaction with nothing personal about it. We break one of God's laws, and then we go to confession to make everything better. Everything is taken care of, right?

But the problem is that sin is *always* personal. When I sin I don't simply break a law, I break the heart of my Father. I break the heart of God who loves me and is always willing my good. I say to my Father that I want to go my own way and that I don't need him.

Anyone who goes to confession to me knows that I generally start confession by praying, "Dear Jesus, by your Holy Spirit, show [name] his sin, not so that he would judge or condemn himself, but so that he would know your mercy." We don't have to sit and be quiet and try to "figure out" our sin. Rather, we need to let God in his goodness reveal our sin to us. It is an act of God's love for us that we are able to see our sin. We can't do this on our own power, but we need God's help.

That's why in my personal prayers, I often ask the Holy Spirit to show me my sin. I must admit there are times I wish I had prayed for a pony instead, because God is generous in answering this prayer. But I know it is good for me to see my sin, and in the depths of my heart, I really do want to know my sin so that I may be converted more and more. God longs to show you your sin, not so you feel guilty or condemned, but so you can know his mercy.

*Shackled*

I was in the Holy Land once, and I was praying early in the morning, reflecting on the Stations of the Cross, trying to prepare my heart for later that day when the group I was leading was going to walk the Via Dolorosa. I didn't expect what happened. As I prayed, I had an image of Jesus walking through the narrow streets of Jerusalem. He was carrying his cross, badly beaten and bloodied. There he was, walking down busy streets with people all around him; some were yelling at him while others were paying no attention at all. Then I saw myself, and then later members of my group, walking up to Jesus and whispering in his ear. I remember not wanting to get very close to him so I would not get his blood all over me, but I needed to get close enough so that others could not hear what I was saying. I approached Jesus, whispering in his ear all of my sins.

"Jesus, you know that there are times when I am going to have too much to drink."

I stepped back to see his reaction. He kept on walking.

"You know that when I am a sophomore, I am going to lie to my mother."

He just kept walking. As this went on, I shared more and more with Jesus. After a while, I began to get upset.

"Jesus, don't you know...?!" He simply looked at me with sorrow in his eyes and pain on his face and kept on walking.

Finally, exasperated, I yelled, "Would you stop! Didn't you hear me? Why are you doing this?"

I will never forget the look on Jesus' face.

He stopped and looked at me, his eyes penetrating my very being, and he simply said, "Because I love you."

And he kept on walking to his death—because he loved me.

This experience had a profound effect on me. In God's grace and love for me, he had allowed me to have a glimpse of the effect of my sin. My sin isn't simply breaking some kind of impersonal, divine rule. Rather, it is an intensely personal offense against the God who created and sustains me. It is a breach in my relationship with Christ, who only wants my good and happiness. My sin is the eternal cause of Christ's suffering.

We were not created to sin, you know. This was not a part of the original design. If you want to get a reprimand from me, then you should begin your confession; "Bless me Father, for I have sinned, but I am only human." That is a lie. You did not sin because you were human. Sin is not human. It is actually *de*humanizing. If we assert that sin is human, then Jesus could not be fully human, because he never sinned. The same could be said for Our Lady who was only human and never sinned. No, when we sin we really do become less human.

Sin not only turns us from our God, but it also turns us from ourselves. As we sin, we become less and less what God created us to be and, in our sin, we slowly begin to die. Sin stops you from being the person you were created to be. It binds you, inhibits you, slowly hardens your heart and numbs your spirit. If you keep sinning, ultimately you get used to it. It is generally true that when a person commits a sin once, it becomes easier to commit it again and again and again. Slowly one becomes blind to the effects of sin and it does not seem to matter anymore.

We cannot fall into the attitude that sin just doesn't matter or the belief that sin just isn't such a big deal. It really is a big deal. Our attitude toward our sin is vitally important. This became clear to me once when I was stuck in a hotel in Texas. Channel surfing, I stopped at a program that featured a Protestant preacher and listened for a very few minutes. He said something that has stayed with me: "God is not as concerned with our sin itself as he is with our *attitude* toward our sin." I think he may be on to something. If we have a laissez-faire attitude toward our sin and act as if it does not matter, then we are never going to move out of it. If our attitude does not become more like Christ's, then we will never be able to live and love like he does (see Philippians 2:5). Unless our hearts and our attitudes toward our sin change, we will always be slaves to sin.

We see it all the time around us. Whether it is lying or cheating, gossiping, maligning people in the office, pride, impatience, arrogance, lack of respect for parents, drunkenness, impurity, adultery, fornication, jealousy, envy, gluttony and anger or a million other things, sins all have eternal consequences. Sin matters. People are slaves to their sin, and they don't even know it. We need to know our sin. We need to beg God to show it to us.

Now, hear me well: I'm not recommending that you ask

God to show you your sin so that you will feel horrible and full of guilt and despair. Rather, you need to ask God, in his love, to show you your sin so that it may be rooted out of your life and so that you can experience his love and mercy. If you do not know your sin then you will continue to live in your sin. If you live in your sin then you will die in your sin. If you die in your sin, well, you know how that goes.

One time, when I finished a talk on sin, a young man approached me and asked if we could talk. We walked behind the stage and he just looked at me. He was dressed in black jeans and a white T-shirt, with his baseball cap on backward. He was a tough-looking kid, but I could tell by his eyes that he was holding back tears.

"Why didn't anyone tell me that before?"

"What?" I asked.

"All that. That pornography and masturbation is a sin. That getting drunk is a sin. That sin was as horrible as it is. Why didn't anyone tell me this?"

Now, I am going to guess that others had probably told him this before, but in a moment of grace, God touched this young man's heart in such a way that he really understood the nature of his sin. He began to cry, and I prayed as he did. He was starting to experience freedom.

So it is kind of a paradox, but coming to know our sin really is a freeing experience. Sin keeps eating at us and deep inside we know that something is wrong. It's kind of like when you leave the house and know that you have forgotten something but you just don't know what it is. You know something is wrong, but often just can't put your finger on it. The moment we become aware of our sin really is a moment of grace and profound wonder.

But becoming aware of our sin is only the first step. We must also be freed from it.

I don't know why, but some people want to hold on to their sin. If you think about it, our sin is the only thing we possess that God did not give us, so I guess some people figure it *belongs* to them, and they don't want to give it up. This is, of course, crazy. God asks us to give him our sin—so that he can give us his forgiveness. Believe me, this is a really good trade. I strongly encourage you to take God up on this.

For other people, the real stumbling block is not the issue of whether or not God will forgive them, but whether or not they will forgive themselves. They are so very bound by things they did in the past, that they have a terrible time forgiving themselves. Is this your situation? You need to know that, in order to be free, you must be able to forgive yourself of your past sins. God forgives you, so how can you not forgive yourself? Maybe you should take some time just to be quiet and pray. Ask God to bring to mind those things that you need to forgive yourself for. When memories come to mind, simply say, "I forgive myself for..." Remember, forgiveness is an act of your will; it is a choice. Based on the fact that God forgives me, I choose to forgive others and myself. It is a decision and an act of the will, not a feeling. If I only forgave when I felt like doing it, I would do very little forgiving. A feeling of peace may follow my decision to forgive others or myself, but it rarely precedes it.

*Let's Make a Deal*

I have experienced freedom the most intensely when I was personally repenting for my sin or hearing confessions of those who were making a good confession. To be able to see my sins and failings clearly and offer them to the Father, knowing that he is not going to turn away but rather is going to offer me forgiveness, is an amazing, beautiful gift. At last, repenting of sin does have to be like admitting defeat or surrendering to the enemy, but it really can be a place of refreshment. It can be a place where we can finally catch our breath, recognizing that repentance and confession have become a safe place, a place of comfort.

One of my greatest joys as a priest is to be the one who is present when a person offers his or her sin and brokenness to God and asks to be reconciled to him. A priest friend of mine has reminded me that this is the sacrament of reconciliation, not the sacrament of sin. Can we keep this in mind? It is right for us to focus on our sin, but the real reason we go to confession is to be reconciled. It is such a blessing to be able to witness this in action; I am permitted to be present when the God of the universe is reconciled with his son or daughter.

As a priest, I can usually tell when someone "gets it," that is, when that person really understands that nature of his or her sin and how this offends God and also exhibits a wholehearted desire to be in union with God. What a difference between someone humbly coming before God like that and someone reading off the shopping-list type of confession. When someone begins with a slight hesitation of voice, whispering, "Bless me, Father, for I have sinned. I have broken the heart of God...." Bless God, now let's begin.

This is such freedom. We get so tired trying to hold everything together or trying to be perfect. What freedom there is to be able to go before God just as we are, declaring, "Here I am, sinful, broken and scared. Forgive me. Breathe your very life into me." There, at that place and time, is freedom.

## JOURNEY TO GOD'S HEART

*Listening:*
Luke 23:34–46

*Reflecting:*
How do you experience the weight of your sin?
What will it mean for you to truly repent?

*Conversing:*
"Jesus, show me the ways I walk away from you."
"Jesus, I wish you would free me from..."

## CHAPTER FIVE

## FREEDOM WON

BEFORE JESUS WAS BORN, WHEN THE LOCAL PEOPLE WERE BENT OUT of shape that Elizabeth was going to name her son John, the Holy Spirit filled her husband Zachariah and freed him from his inability to speak. Anointed with the Spirit, he prophesied that Jesus had come to set his people free, to free his people from their enemies and oppressors and to provide his people with the freedom to worship without fear.

Zachariah proclaimed:

> Blessed be the Lord the God of Israel, he has come to set his people free.... This was the oath he swore to our father Abraham; to set us free from the hands of our enemies, free to worship him without fear, holy and righteous in his sight all the days of our life. (Luke 1:68, 70–72, Divine Office translation)

As Zachariah's words reveal, humanity was and is powerless. We human beings could not, cannot save ourselves. Try as I might, I am not able to free myself from the plague of sin and death.

It was God himself who had to reach out to save us. Whether it was through Moses, David, Isaiah or Ezekiel, God was reaching out to his people in order to free them. The Old Testament tells the story of God longing to bring his people back to himself, to bring them out of slavery. The people of the Old Testament did experience a measure of freedom. However, it was incomplete and temporary. The Israelites found freedom from Egyptian oppression. But, as has been noted, one can be free from tyranny and domination and still not be really free, still be bound by sin, fear, anger and death.

The freedom God intended to bring was the original freedom he had given humanity at creation. This type of freedom now had to come at a great price, the sacrificial offering of God himself.

In his brief prophetic statement, Zachariah pointed to one of the central points of Jesus' mission: freedom. Jesus was going to finally and definitively set his people free. He would do this by the power of his Word along with the way he lived and ultimately died.

Jesus himself was free. One needs only to spend a few minutes with the Scriptures to recognize that the way Jesus lived was different. He always did what he knew to be right regardless of how others might react. He was not burdened by what others thought of him. Whether it was dining with sinners and prostitutes or healing on the Sabbath, it was clear that Jesus was not going to be bound by anyone's preconceived notions or expectations.

Jesus was fully aware that freedom was a significant part of his mission. In the beginning of the fourth chapter of

Luke, we find Jesus being led by the Spirit into the desert. There we read of Jesus being tempted by the devil. The Scripture states that when the devil had finished tempting him, Jesus returned to his hometown of Nazareth where, filled with the Holy Spirit, he entered the synagogue on the Sabbath.

When Jesus entered the synagogue,

> He stood up to read and was handed a scroll of the prophet Isaiah. He unrolled the scroll and found the passage where it was written:
>
> "The Spirit of the Lord is upon me,
>     because he has anointed me
>         to bring glad tidings to the poor.
> He has sent me to proclaim liberty to captives
>     and recovery of sight to the blind,
>         to let the oppressed go free,
> and to proclaim a year acceptable to the Lord."
>
> Rolling up the scroll, he handed it back to the attendant and sat down, and the eyes of all in the synagogue looked intently at him. He said to them, "Today this scripture passage is fulfilled in your hearing." (Luke 4:16–21)

I can only imagine what must have gone through the minds and hearts of those blessed enough to be in the synagogue that morning. What was it like to hear the Word proclaim the Word? What a grace to see Jesus standing before them reading and speaking about the sacred text. What must have gone through their minds when he said, "Today, this scripture passage is fulfilled in your hearing"? Jesus had just said that *he* is the fulfillment of all the hopes and dreams of the people of the Old Testament. Talk about being at the right place at the right time!

This was the beginning of Jesus' public ministry, the inauguration, if you will. Jesus was beginning his ministry by boldly proclaiming that God had anointed him to bring freedom: "He has sent me to proclaim liberty to captives and recovery of sight to the blind, to let the oppressed go free, and to proclaim a year acceptable to the Lord" (Luke 4:18).

Don't read this Scripture passage and miss the fact that it is meant for us today just as much as it was meant for the people in Jesus' hometown. *We* are the captive, the blind and the oppressed that Jesus came to bring freedom to. Jesus came to bring freedom not only to those who were listening to him that day, but to you and me as well. Jesus came so *I* would not be blind anymore. He came so that *you* would be able to see even in the midst of darkness. When Jesus said that he had come to free the captive, he was thinking of all of the people who heard him, and he was also thinking of you and me.

Jesus has always wanted to free you from whatever it is that cages you. Those fears that constantly bombard you? Jesus came to free you from them. Jesus' whole life and his ministry are all about freedom, and he's still in the freedom business today.

*Broken Free*

In the eighth chapter of John, Jesus pointed out how bound his followers really were. Jesus told them:

> "If you remain in my word, you will truly be my disciples, and you will know the truth, and the truth will set you free." They answered him, "We are descendants of Abraham and have never been enslaved to anyone. How can you say, 'You will become free'?" Jesus answered them, "Amen, amen, I say to you, everyone who commits sin is a slave of sin. A slave does not remain in a household forever, but a son always remains. So if a son frees you, then you will truly be free. I know that you are descendants of Abraham. But you are trying to kill me, because my word has no room among you." (John 8:31–37)

Jesus' followers resisted his assertion that they are not free. "We have never been enslaved by anyone." While it was true that the Jewish people had been controlled and dominated by outside forces, they never considered themselves "slaves," believing rather that, as God's chosen people, they were free. So when Jesus told them that they were, in fact, slaves, they took offense. However, Jesus wasn't referring to political slavery. The slavery to which Jesus was referring was much more serious, much more deadly. He was stating that the people were slaves to sin and this slavery would ultimately cause their death. "Amen, amen...everyone who commits sin is a slave to sin" (John 8:34).

We modern-day followers of Jesus also know this to be the case, if we allow ourselves to think about it. Until we experience the freedom that Christ brings, we truly are slaves to our sins and passions. Paul's famous dilemma in the seventh chapter of Romans rings true for us. "What I do, I do not understand. For I do not do what I want, but I do what I hate.... So now it is no longer I who do it, but sin that dwells in me" (Romans 7:15, 17). What person has not at some point asked himself or herself the same questions. We say, "Why did I do that? Why did I say that? Why didn't I? Why? How can I get out of this mess?"

This is at the very heart of why Jesus came to earth. We couldn't break free, so he came to free us from the midst of our sin. The Scripture says:

> Indeed, only with difficulty does one die for a just person, though perhaps for a good person one might even find courage to die. But God proves his love for us in that while we were still sinners Christ died for us. (Romans 5:7–8)

I find this text haunting. God proves his love for me? You've got to be kidding. What did he have to prove to me? It is I who should be proving my love for God. I am the fickle one. I am the one who walks away time and time again. I am the one who says no to his love and his grace. He proves his love for me? And if this is not enough, he proves his love while I am a sinner. He didn't even wait until I got my act together. I suppose it's because that probably never would have happened.

Your spiritual life radically changes the instant you come to realize that you are the guilty one; that you are the one who deserves the death sentence. The moment I realize Jesus took my place, I understand what it means that I have been saved. Jesus saved us from pain and death. He freed us from a life of sin and destruction and opened for us the kingdom of his Father. This is good news!

The good news is that you don't have to be a slave to sin. It is possible to be freed from behavior that is destructive. I know that you have struggled with the same sin for five, ten or thirty years but there is freedom and you need to claim it. Paul clearly states this when writing to the Romans:

> For when you were slaves of sin, you were free from righteousness. But what profit did you get then from the things of which you are now ashamed? For the end of those things is death. But now that you have been *freed* from sin and have become slaves of God, the benefit that you have leads to sanctification, and its end is eternal life. For the wages of sin is death, but the gift of God is eternal life in Christ Jesus our Lord. (Romans 6:20–23, emphasis mine)

In Christ, we have been given the gift of freedom from our sin. Jesus shed his blood so that I would be free to love him and be loved by him and inherit eternal life. We must stand on this rock of truth. Jesus' death and resurrection frees us from the power of sin and death. You do not have to be held captive any longer. "He himself bore our sins in his body upon the cross, so that, free from sin, we might live for righteousness. By his wounds you have been healed" (1 Peter 2:24). Bless God, we are free.

*Free to Worship*

In Jesus' time, being faithful to God felt like a burden to many people. Over the centuries, laws had been developed along with the Ten Commandments that articulated exactly how people were to live their faith. It became almost impossible to follow every rule and regulation, and people were always fearful of breaking the Law and thus losing the favor of God. Certain religious leaders followed the Law in such a way as to place undue burdens on others. To these people Jesus was very stern. "Woe also to you scholars of the law! You impose on people burdens hard to carry, but you yourselves do not lift one finger to touch them" (Luke 11:46). Jesus also chastises these same leaders for disregarding God's commands while clinging to human traditions (see Mark 7:8). It was not that Jesus had something against the Law, but he objected to the spirit of legalism that caused the religious leaders to demand unreasonable and impossible obedience from their flock. He was going to change this.

In all likelihood, there was a "heaviness" to living the faith. The people constantly feared breaking a law or doing something that would make them ritually impure. I imagine that this created a type of adversarial relationship between God and the people, as if God were policing their every move, ready to punish them for any misstep.

That's not the kind of God we have.

The reason I say it in those words is because God said it to me that way a long time ago. When I was younger, my older brother was involved in some pretty destructive behavior. I was a kid and remember praying that God would do something to him to show him that the way he was living was wrong. A day or two after making this prayer, my family got a phone call from the fire department. My brother had been in an accident. He had been working on a car and it had fallen off the jack, breaking his skull. As it turned out, he was OK, but I was a mess. Imagine what goes through the mind of a kid: I say my prayer and then a car falls on my brother. God means business. Do not tick him off. (Or me, for that matter.)

For the longest time and honestly for the most part without being aware of it, I held on to an understanding that God was out to get us. If any of us did something wrong, something bad was going to happen. If something went wrong, I would wonder who did what to cause it. One evening years later I was praying, and God brought this memory back to me. I began to understand how I was viewing God. I heard God say to me, "Dave, *that is not the kind of God that I am.* I am loving and kind, and I am not out to get you." At that moment, I broke down. I hadn't fully understood the weight I had been carrying. I had been bound for so long with this warped image of a God who was waiting for me to make a mistake so he could punish me. Well, that is not the kind of God we have. At that moment I saw God more clearly than ever before. There was a physical sense of something being taken away from me. A weight was removed from my heart that had burdened me for so long.

Paul sums this up in one of my favorite Scriptures:

If God is for us, who can be against us? He who did not spare his own Son but handed him over for us all, how will he not also give us everything else along with him?

Who will bring a charge against God's chosen ones? It is God who acquits us. Who will condemn? It is Christ [Jesus] who died, rather, was raised, who also is at the right hand of God, who indeed intercedes for us. What will separate us from the love of Christ? Will anguish, or distress, or persecution, or famine, or nakedness, or peril, or the sword? As it is written:

"For your sake we are being slain all the day;
  we are looked upon as sheep to be slaughtered."

No, in all these things we conquer overwhelmingly through him who loved us. For I am convinced that neither death, nor life, nor angels, nor principalities, nor present things, nor future things, nor powers, nor height, nor depth, nor any other creature will be able to separate us from the love of God in Christ Jesus our Lord. (Romans 8:31–39)

In Jesus, we have an entirely new way of looking at God. We have a God who is *for* us, a God who is on our side. Sit with that for a moment. God is on your side. It is not you against him. Rather, he is for you. He has always been on your side. When everyone seemed against you or out to get you, God was there. When no one seemed to notice you or recognize something special that you had done, God noticed. When it felt like the world was tearing you down at every turn, God was present to pick us back up. He was always there for you and he still is. To the degree we come to experience this God, we are truly free to worship God without fear. Now I can understand more fully what John was saying when he stated "perfect love drives out fear" (1 John 4:18). It's not *my* perfect love; it is God's. I really don't have anything to be afraid of.

### Abba, Father

This is most clearly shown to us as Jesus reveals to us a God we can call "Father." He's not some God who is distant and uninterested in us, but rather a God who runs to greet us whenever we return home. This is a radically new understanding of God, one that got Jesus in trouble with the religious leaders of his day. But it is keenly essential for us. If God is our Father, then it stands to reason that we are his sons and daughters. Paul wrote this in his Letter to the Romans:

> For you did not receive a spirit of slavery to fall back into fear, but you received a spirit of adoption, through which we cry, *Abba* "Father!" The Spirit itself bears witness with our spirit that we are children of God. (Romans 8:15–16)

Once I was talking with a teenage boy from Minnesota about God as Father. He blurted out, "My dad isn't much of a father. You want to know something? I have never done anything alone with my dad. One time we were going to go hunting together and we were packed and ready to go but the weather looked bad. My dad decided that we would go another day when the weather got better. I'm still waiting."

My experience was quite the opposite. My father is my best friend and teacher. I remember one time when I was in the eighth grade, I was with my dad in the car and I was trying to impress him with what I had learned in school that day. I told him something about Pikes Peak and he asked me a follow-up question to which I had no earthly idea of the answer. He must have known what I was trying to do because he said, "Dave, you don't have to impress me or your mother; we love you for who you are, not for what you know." This was pretty good news, given that I did not know very much.

I am fully aware that my experience is not the experience of many people and that the idea of a loving Father God is extremely foreign to them. Time and time again, I have heard statements such as, "If God is like *my* father, I'll pass." But Jesus wants to change this; he wants to free you from the false understandings of what it means to have God as Father. Your Father in heaven is not critical and insensitive; rather he "is gracious and merciful, slow to anger and abounding in love" (Psalm 145:8). God our Father never once missed a recital or that really important game. God the Father is so interested in you that "[e]ven all the hairs of your head are counted. So do not be afraid; you are worth more than many sparrows" (Matthew 10:30–31).

Coming to understand that we have a God who is our defender and our protector brings great joy and freedom to us. We have a Father in heaven who is going to watch over us and take care of us. We have a God who cares for us enough to chastise us when necessary, but he always does it in love and not anger (see Revelation 3:19). Jesus helps reveal a caring, loving God whom we are free to worship. We do not have to be afraid to go before him the way Dorothy feared approaching the Wizard of Oz. Rather, we can approach the Father knowing of his tenderness and love. What freedom there is in being able to draw near to a God who also happens to be our Father.

## The Price Is Right

All of this came at a price. Saint Mark tells us, "For the Son of Man did not come to be served but to serve and to give his life as a ransom for many" (Mark 10:45). What a ransom! Your life is so precious and valuable that only Christ himself could pay an adequate sum for it. The blood of an animal was not enough to set you free. Only Christ's blood, freely offered, would pay the debt. The blood price was freely paid by Christ: "This is why the Father loves me, because I lay down my life in order to take it up again. No one takes it from me, but I lay it down on my own" (John 10:17–18). Jesus was not forced or coerced, nor did he do it because he was under duress. He was totally free when he gave his life for us. Jesus died as he had lived: fully free. Think about the overwhelming scene of Jesus being tortured, beaten, hanging exposed from a piece of wood for all the world to see. This was one of the greatest acts of freedom known to man.

"Father, forgive them, they know not what they do" (Luke 23:34). Only a man absolutely and totally free would have been able, in the middle of being crucified, to utter such a thing. Jesus looked into the eyes of his executioners and advocated for their forgiveness—what an unbelievable act of freedom. Christ is offering us the same type of freedom. Jesus Christ is offering us a whole new way of living, a new way of loving. He is making it possible for us to forgive anyone—even our own executioners, if it comes to that. He is inviting us to a freedom that, no matter the circumstances, can never be taken away.

It is one thing to be freed by Moses or David or any other of the Old Testament figures. It is quite another to be freed by the Son. Jesus says in the Gospel that when the son sets you free you are really free (see John 8:36). This is for you, and you need to be able to hear Jesus say it to you. Become still and quiet and in the depths of your heart and allow Jesus to show you how and where you are bound. Then he can speak a word of freedom to your particular bondage.

I can tell you that God wants you to be free. Your spouse can tell you that God wants you to be free. But it is something altogether different to hear the Son himself tell you that you *are* free.

When Jesus speaks a word of freedom to your heart, his word carries undeniable power. When I, Father Dave, tell you that you can be free, you may truly want to believe me, but in your heart you may wonder if I really know. When Christ tells you that you can be free, you have it on the authority of someone who really knows. This word of freedom is coming from a man whom not even death could bind. Yes, this word comes from Jesus Christ our Lord, the very source of freedom.

## JOURNEY TO GOD'S HEART

*Listening:*
John 10:9–18

*Reflecting:*
In what way are you blind, crippled or imprisoned?
How would your life look different if you loved
God wholeheartedly and Jesus alone were at
the center of your heart?

*Conversing:*
"Jesus, I believe you are trying to tell me..."
"Jesus, once again I surrender my heart to you; now
please give me yours."

## CHAPTER SIX

## FREEDOM'S GATEWAY

I REMEMBER THE FIRST TIME I MET LISA. IT WAS ONE OF THOSE beautiful days that make being on a college campus so wonderful. The students were enjoying the weather, lying on the grass studying (or at least lying on the grass with books in front of them). I was walking outside from my office to the chapel when a woman whom I had never met ran up to me, gave me an enthusiastic hug and told me she loved me. Not a bad introduction. It turns out that two of Lisa's children were attending Franciscan University and she and her husband Danny were visiting them.

Lisa and I became fast friends. (Heck, after such an introduction how could we not?) Each time Lisa visited campus, she would bring me some little gift. Whether it was a Fighting Irish music box or homemade applesauce, Lisa never seemed to come to my office or to the friary empty-handed. She was always thinking about others and looking for little things she could do to brighten someone's day. She had a love of life that was contagious.

In November, about a year after our first meeting, Lisa's daughter informed me that her mom had been diagnosed with cancer. About six months later, I was able to visit the family for a few days. I remember talking with Lisa about her being healed. "Father Dave, if I am healed, great. If not, I get to be with Jesus. I win either way." Wow, what a great attitude.

Later that day I sat in on a family meeting with a social worker. Lisa began to talk about things she wanted to have happen before she died. She said, "I hope it's before school starts. It would be such an inconvenience if the kids were in school." Even as she approached death, Lisa was always thinking about others. She was comforting her family and supporting them. To me, this seemed backward.

One of the evenings during my stay, I joined the family for their nightly rosary walk. By this time Lisa could no longer walk, so we all took turns pushing her wheelchair. At one point, her husband started running while pushing Lisa. She was giggling and squealing like a five-year-old girl whose father is pushing her on a swing. I was walking behind, and I saw her with her arms stretched out as if she were flying. She had a rosary dangling from her left hand, and all of this appeared in front of a backdrop of a glowing pink horizon and the setting sun. I thought to myself, *She's dying, yet she's laughing.*

Lisa and I had the opportunity to talk a couple of times during my visit. We talked about her cancer and her impending death. She talked about the things she was not going to be able to see, such as her daughter's wedding, grandkids or her sons' ordinations. I offered the comment that it must be terribly difficult. She looked at me with kind of a puzzled gaze and said, "Father Dave, it's only my cross." It was the way she said it, so matter-of-factly: "It's only my cross." We all have crosses and this was Lisa's; she was going to die far too young.

Only her cross...a cross that had caused her tremendous suffering, a cross that had caused so much pain, a cross that was going to cause her death, a cross that was going to take her from her family much too soon. "Father Dave, it's only my cross." I prayed with Lisa that day, heard her confession and later we celebrated Mass in her living room. It would be Lisa's last Eucharistic Celebration. She died a few weeks later. She died a free woman.

Lisa was free. She was free in her life and she was free in her death. You see, Lisa taught me a priceless lesson about faith, death, life and freedom. As I said at her funeral Mass, the cancer caused Lisa's death, but it never took her life. And this was true. Lisa was so alive because she understood that life comes through the cross and through suffering. She was able to connect her suffering with the suffering of Jesus and in this she experienced the freedom Christ had won for her.

This is an essential reality of our faith. When Jesus embraced his cross, he gave life to the entire world. When each of us is able to embrace our own cross, we receive life and from this we give life to those with whom we come in contact. By our ability to embrace our crosses, we help to liberate all we meet. In suffering and embracing our crosses, we discover Jesus who is the source of freedom. In our suffering, we are able to discover a depth of God that is impossible to find or experience apart from such suffering. Amazing as it is, our crosses and sufferings become our pathway to Jesus. They can become our means of sanctification. They help us to be holy. Suffering really is the gateway to freedom.

*Life Is Tough*

We would be a lot happier if we would take this line to heart: *Life is hard.* It's just that simple. Somewhere along the line, most of us bought into the lie that tells us life is supposed to be easy. It is not easy. The real world is not like one of a million sitcoms, where the day's problems are happily resolved in about twenty-four minutes. Life simply isn't like that. It is difficult, really hard. I suppose at times we need to be reminded that Jesus invited us to pick up our crosses, not our beach chairs.

It's hard to accept the fact that life is hard. We want it to be easy so that we don't have to hurt. Don't get me wrong; I am not out there looking for suffering. The problem is that in our desire for life to be easy we spend a lot of time ignoring or running from the reality that is life.

We are not much different from the people Moses led out of slavery. They thought that everything was going to be easy after they were freed from the pharaoh. After journeying for some time, though, the people got frustrated with Moses and with God. Moses intervened on behalf of the people, and God in his goodness provided manna for the people to eat. But soon, that, too, was not good enough. They complained more:

"Why have you brought us up from Egypt to die in this desert, where there is no food or water? We are disgusted with this wretched food!" In punishment the LORD sent among the people saraph serpents, which bit the people so that many of them died. Then the people came to Moses and said, "We have sinned in complaining against the LORD and you. Pray the LORD to take the serpents from us." So Moses prayed for the people, and the Lord said to Moses, "Make a saraph and mount it on a pole, and if anyone who has been bitten looks at it, he will recover." Moses accordingly made a bronze serpent and mounted it on a pole, and whenever anyone who had been bitten by a serpent looked at the bronze serpent, he recovered. (Numbers 21:5–9)

This is a remarkable story and it provides us one of the greatest keys to healing and freedom. Imagine what the people must have thought when Moses told them to take the serpent and mount it on a pole. They were supposed to look at the very thing that had caused their pain and this was now going to heal them? Really now, what must they have thought? *Moses has finally lost it. We should have stayed with the pharaoh.* The serpent was the source of their pain. The people were doing everything in their power to get away from it and now Moses is asking them to stop and look at it? This really was amazing. The source of their pain and death became the source of their healing.

Jesus reiterated this in the third chapter of John. "And just as Moses lifted up the serpent in the desert, so must the Son of Man be lifted up, so that everyone who believes in him may have eternal life" (John 3:14–15).

In the same way that the people who were suffering looked at the serpent and were healed, we look at Jesus lifted on the cross and we can be made whole. But this is difficult. Too often we want to look away from the cross. We don't want to look at his cross and we don't want to look at our own crosses. We don't want to stop and look. All too often we prefer to ignore our crosses in hopes that they will magically go away. But they won't. Eventually, we will have to stop and look. It's a paradox. By looking at the cross of Jesus and at my own cross, I am healed.

There are things in your life that you don't really want to look at. Once a student said to me, "Father, I am afraid if I really look at this [her source of suffering], I will start crying and never stop." She was not being some overly dramatic college kid. For years she had tried with all of her might to forget the awful things that had happened to her. She, like so many people, stayed busy all the time for fear of what she would hear or see if she stopped or slowed down.

Or there are those like Brad in Tampa who told me, "Father, I know drugs and alcohol are ruining me. But they allow me to escape and for a few minutes I don't have to look at the pain." Does this sound familiar? I know the thought of you stopping and looking at the things you have tried so hard to forget is really, really scary. Perhaps it is the abuse you received when you were a child, the abuse you caused, your unfaithfulness, the death of a loved one, betrayal, hate or a million other things. But you can't keep running from it, whatever it is. It will always catch up to you. It will always come out someplace in your life. Whether it is drinking too much, impatience, anger or addiction, it just can't be ignored. It must be looked at. But here is a miraculous reality: The place of your suffering can become your place of healing. When you stop and look at your suffering, you are invited to find Jesus there.

*Light Out of Darkness*

Lest we forget, our redemption, our freedom, was won for us on a cross by a bloody, suffering Messiah. I don't know how fully we comprehend the horror of the cross. Oddly, we have made our crosses pretty. We hear, "Oh, that is such a beautiful cross."

"Why, thank you. I got it for 50 percent off at Wal-Mart."

"It's simply beautiful, so unique. I like the way the little red rubies are placed where the nails usually are."

"Yes, and if the light hits it just right, they really sparkle."

I mean, I understand it, but it's just kind of odd. Perhaps this represents part of our desire to avoid crosses in general. By making them pretty we are able to deal with them better. (I also fully understand that if one gets past the visible horror of a cross and comes to understand what Jesus did for us there, it *is* beautiful.)

We must remember that it is through a *cross* that God chose to save you. If you can get past the fear of looking at it, you will discover that you actually find Jesus there. The cross is not some empty, meaningless monument commemorating the death of Jesus. Rather it is a source of hope revealing the power of life, the supremacy of light.

Because of the cross, light always wins. The light comes from the darkness. Remember that Jesus rose out of darkness, that "the light shines in the darkness, / and the darkness has not overcome it" (John 1:5). The cross and your suffering are not to be feared, but you are invited to embrace them.

It is impossible to embrace your cross without also embracing Jesus. Jesus is eternally there. For this reason, you do not have to be afraid to embrace the cross. When you are able to do this, you discover that you are not alone. This is good news. God is there.

I did not always understand this. To be perfectly honest, I know that I still have only the slightest insight here, but I hope I am learning. Once again, I recall my time in seminary when I was experiencing such difficulty. As I have mentioned, my goddaughter had recently died, and I had just completed a summer internship working at Children's Hospital in Washington, D.C. For twelve weeks I worked as a chaplain in the neonatal intensive care unit as well as the pediatric intensive care unit. During those weeks I sat with dozens of people as their sons and daughters died. I simply was not equipped to answer the question of a twenty-six-year-old mother holding her child who had just died: "Why did God let this happen? I prayed. I thought God would want to heal my baby."

Sure, I gave some answers that may or may not have helped, but so often I went home to the friary chapel and asked God exactly the same question. Honestly, is there an answer that really would make sense at a time like that?

"Oh, now I understand, now it all makes sense. Thank you so much." It was all so confusing, so dark. And if I didn't have all the answers as a seminarian, what kind of priest was I going to be?

All this time, God seemed distant. Prayer, Mass, everything felt foreign to me. For a young man who was preparing to be a priest, this was terribly frightening. I felt as if I was caught in a fog, not able to see or feel anything.

"God, if you would take away the haze so that I can see you, everything will be OK. Please, Lord, just let me see you so that I can understand." As I have already shared, God did break through to me on that Thursday evening in the chapel. He told me that I was loved, but he also revealed more than that. After having heard God tell me that he loved me, I asked him to take away the fog so that I would be more able to see him. Then I felt that God said to me, "Dave, don't you know that I am in the fog?"

To which I replied, "Well, um, no."

God was in the middle of my fog? I thought that I had to get over the pain and hurt so that I would be able to see and experience God again, but he showed me that he actually wanted me to see and experience him in the *middle* of the pain and suffering. It wasn't about "getting over it," but rather about stopping, looking at the pain and being in it, then allowing God to show himself to me in the midst of it.

To this day, that evening was one of the most profound experiences of God I have ever had. I stopped asking him to take away the pain and asked him to show me his face in the middle of it. My life was never the same.

There is unbelievable freedom when you are able to stop running from your suffering and pain and let God show himself to you in the middle of it. It is not in getting rid of your suffering that you are free; rather it is in embracing it. Your life will become radically different when you find God in the midst of your hurt. When you can honestly say that you see God's love as you look upon his cross, you are moving toward a freedom that this world can never take away.

I know that this sounds crazy. I continually go back to what Saint Paul said:

> For Jews demand signs and Greeks look for wisdom, but we proclaim Christ crucified, a stumbling block to Jews and foolishness to Gentiles, but to those who are called, Jews and Greeks alike, Christ the power of God and the wisdom of God. (1 Corinthians 1:22–24)

If I am able to find God's love in the darkest place known to man, the crucifixion, then I can find him in the middle of my darkest hour. Whether it's in a neonatal intensive care unit, Lisa's living room or your greatest struggle, Christ is there. There is no place so dark that God's light cannot illuminate it. In the darkest dark that you can imagine, even the smallest light shatters the darkness. That light is God.

## Suffering's Gift

I am aware that it requires a shift in how we think in order to believe this. We live in a world that tries to sell us on the idea that we should have no suffering, no pain. We have pain medication for every imaginable ache. Don't get me wrong, I'm not against medicine; I am a doctor's son. But suffering teaches us about life, and it can help us become more grounded. I love what Pope John Paul II said regarding suffering:

> In suffering we seem to attain a better grasp of the fundamental meaning of the proportions which in general escape our attention. We seem to experience more deeply the fragility of our existence and hence the mystery of our creation, the responsibility for life, the sense of good and evil, and finally the ineffable majesty of God.[1]

In suffering we are able to not only experience God but also discover our very selves. By embracing suffering we can actually become more human. I used to think that we suffered because Jesus suffered, but I no longer think this. I believe it is the other way around. Jesus suffered because we suffer. Suffering really is a part of our human condition, but it didn't have to be part of his. In my mind this makes what Jesus did all the more remarkable. Jesus freely took on humanity, along with our suffering, and he embraced human frailty. In doing this, he provided meaning to our suffering and also to our very existence. He sanctified it and thereby freed us from its curse. Because of the work of Christ, rather than trying to escape suffering, we may be formed by it.

I love the idea expressed by French poet Léon Bloy that there are places in our poor hearts which do not yet exist and into which suffering must enter so that they may. Suffering allows us to become more compassionate, understanding and loving. Our hearts are formed through suffering. Suffering can actually become a gift. When this happens, we move into the freedom that I believe God intends for us.

I met someone who experienced this firsthand. He was a priest in Africa, and I met him while I was doing evangelization work there. The local bishop wanted me to pray with a priest friend of his who had recently been struck with a mysterious muscular disease. Slowly, his friend was losing the use of the muscles in his legs. As soon as I began talking and praying with Father Joe, I was relatively certain that God was not going to heal him. I asked the bishop if I could have some time alone with Father Joe. Father began to share with me what God was teaching him through the illness. He stated that he was praying in a much deeper and more profound way and that God was allowing him to become more detached from the world and much more dependent on him. He said he was now more able to connect with his congregation in new and profound ways. He was feeling an unbelievable closeness to God. While I was talking with Father, I had the overwhelming desire to pray that God *not* heal him. Through his experience of suffering, Father Joe was personally being transformed, as was his ministry. I did not want that to be taken away from him. In the end, instead of praying for healing, I rejoiced at what God was doing in Father Joe and I prayed that God's will be done.

Now that experience may be a little unusual, but rest assured that I am not clueless nor am I living in some pipe dream. I am fully aware that not all people who experience suffering and loss have this profound mystical experience of God. I know that many people become angry and bitter due to the suffering or pain that they have experienced. Many people have to travel through this valley often, without realizing that if they persevere, God will draw them out of the darkness.

Some people feel that there is a prerequisite to being healed or set free. They feel they need to be able to "forget what happened" first. This simply isn't true. The experiences of many people are so difficult and so traumatic that there is no way they will ever forget what happened. There is also no way for them to "go back and change things." Holding on to this desire is a recipe for more and more frustration. The event has taken place; therefore the origin of the bondage will always be there. But what can change is how we live today. Too many people are bound by fear and pain from events that happened dozens of years ago. God wants to heal that. He is not going to take away the event or the circumstances that caused our pain, but we can be freed from the effects. We can be freed from the anger, hatred or distrust we experience due to some painful experience.

Finally, many people become angry because they feel as if they have to understand *why*. I remember talking with a priest when I was young, and he was sharing with me a time in his life that was really very difficult. He asked God, "Why me?" to which he heard God respond, "Why *not* you?" In that moment of grace, he said, it finally made sense. Who was he to demand that God explain himself, as if God actually owed him an explanation? On the other hand, did he really want someone else to have to bear the suffering that he was experiencing?

Honestly, I find the question "why?" problematic. As my priest friend stated, does God really have to explain himself to me? I think that my asking the question "why?" is like a dog chasing his own tail—it will not get me anywhere. Do I really have to understand all the ways of God? I have become more comfortable with the reality that I simply don't have to understand and that some things just don't make sense.

Rather than asking the question "why?" I try to ask "what?" instead. "What are you doing here God?" "What do you want to show me?" "What do you want to heal in me?" "What do you want to transform?" "What do you want to unite?"

One Easter morning I was praying while reading about the Resurrection in the Gospel of John, and I was struck by John's reaction at seeing the empty tomb (see John 20:1–9). The text states that John looked into the tomb and he believed. It goes on to say that they did not yet understand what it meant to rise from the dead. John did not have to understand in order to believe. John, who was the disciple whom Jesus loved, was consumed by his love for Christ and Christ's love for him. He just saw the empty tomb and he believed.

I really don't understand why bad things happen. I don't know why children are abused. I don't know why loved ones tragically die. I don't know why people hated Jesus so much that they felt he needed to die. But I do know that in the midst of it all, God is present. We do not suffer alone and we do not suffer in vain. To be able to accept this is very freeing.

Finally, another significant thing I have learned is that I don't have to defend God. I have found great freedom in this. He really can take care of himself. I don't have to be able to explain to someone else why God allowed awful things to happen. Why did God allow these things to happen? I don't know, but I do know that God is present in the middle of your pain and that he desires to comfort you and make himself known to you.

Some people actually choose suffering. If we think about it, this is what our fasting and penance is supposed to be about. We choose, on a very small scale, to experience some kind of discomfort, and we offer it to Christ and ask him to unite it with his and make us holy. However, there are people like Saint Maximilian Kolbe who chose to suffer and die so that someone else could live. Kolbe was so at peace that while he was being starved in cellblock 11 at Auschwitz, he would sing songs of praise to God. The guards eventually refused to go near his cell. His joy in suffering was simply too much for them to handle. Kolbe was free.

And then there is Nancy. For the last couple years of her life, Nancy suffered tremendously with cancer. As she was drawing closer to death, the suffering became more profound. The day that she died, people could hear her praying and whispering, "No, no, no."

One of the people with her said, "It is OK, Nancy. Don't be afraid. It is OK to let go."

Nancy responded faintly, "I am not afraid. It's just that

when I die I know I am going to be at peace with Jesus and I want to be able to offer him my sufferings for a little longer." Nancy was a free woman.

### Make It Better

Watch a child. If a little boy falls in the park and scrapes his elbow, he instinctively runs to his father or mother to make it better. The boy doesn't ask why he fell down and got hurt; he just wants to be with his mommy or daddy and he knows it will help. More often than not, the parent can do nothing except gently kiss the bruised elbow and tell the little one that it is going to be OK. The amazing thing is that often this is all the child needs. The kiss doesn't "fix" it; it just lets the little one know that he is loved, he is not alone, and he is going to be OK. Sadly, as we grow up we begin to believe that a little kiss or a mere hug isn't going to fix anything, so we stop asking. And we suffer alone.

God the Father is inviting you to run to him with your cut elbows, broken heart or shattered dreams. No hurt is too little and none is too great. Our loving God will meet you and let you know that you are not alone and that you really are going to be OK. He will whisper in your ear and tell you that you are his and that your pain and suffering do not have to control you. He will remind you that there is freedom and healing and that they are found in his heart. If you allow yourself to be still, you will be able to hear and feel his beating heart. Then, as a baby finds comfort on the chest of her mother, so you will find, in the Father's heart, freedom.

## Journey to God's Heart

*Listening:*
John 20:1–9

*Reflecting:*
Have you made the mistake of thinking that the
easy way is the best way?
Where do you experience darkness, despair, confusion?
What should you do?

*Conversing:*
"Jesus, what is my cross? Have I embraced it?"
"Christ, I invite you to come into the midst
of my darkness..."

## CHAPTER SEVEN

# FREE LIKE A BIRD

*Knock, Knock?*
*Who's There?*
*The Holy Spirit?*
*The Holy Spirit who?*

EXACTLY, AND THAT'S THE PROBLEM. THE THIRD PERSON OF THE Trinity can knock on the door of our hearts, and more often than not we don't answer because we don't recognize the Spirit. Who wants to let a stranger in?

To be free, you must recognize the Holy Spirit and allow him to enter your heart. Saint Paul tells us, "Now the Lord is the Spirit, and where the Spirit of the Lord is, there is freedom" (2 Corinthians 3:17). It can't be more plain and clear than that. If you want to be free, you need the grace of the Holy Spirit in your life.

One of the most important experiences of my life happened in 1985. I spent a year with the National Evangelization Teams (NET), based in St. Paul, Minnesota. NET is an outstanding organization devoted to evangelizing Catholic youth. I was twenty years old and needed a break from college to figure out what God wanted me to do. Serving the Church with NET seemed like a good option.

As my mom and I approached the NET center, she said to me, "You know, this group may be charismatic." I didn't really know what that meant so I asked her to explain. She stated that it was a spirituality that was very open to the Holy Spirit. I asked if I was charismatic. She said, "Well, kind of."

Like a lamb to the slaughter...

That evening I was getting settled and a staff member informed me that there was going to be a prayer meeting that evening and I was welcome to attend. I thought it would be a good idea; I had had a long day and a little quiet time would be nice.

Not so much.

As soon as the first song was over people began shouting and raising their hands and making all kinds of noise, at least that's how it seemed to *me*. I didn't know what was going on. I felt really uncomfortable, like a real outsider, like the only man stuck at a bridal shower. (That is another story for another day.) These people didn't pray like I did. They were saying things that I did not understand. At the end of the songs, they would just keep on singing individual songs and melodies. In the midst of my bewilderment, I found something attractive about what was taking place. I was touched by the freedom with which these people prayed. They didn't seem to be concerned with what the person next to them might think. They were not watching what other people were doing.

(That would have been my job.) There was an excitement about God in this group of people that I had not experienced before. But they were still weird.

The next day I was speaking with a man named Rob, and he asked me when I had been baptized in the Holy Spirit. I didn't know exactly what he meant. Was he up to something? I stated that I had been baptized as a baby, but was rather certain that was not what he was talking about. "No, not baptized like the sacrament, but baptized in the Holy Spirit. When did people pray over you and you came to know the power of God, the power of his Holy Spirit?" I didn't know how to answer. But I was pretty sure I hadn't experienced what he was talking about and I was very certain that Rob was giving me the heebie-jeebies. He looked at me with this look that reminded me of the witch in the *Wizard of Oz*: "I'll get you, my pretty...."

Then he said to me, "Well, we need to pray over you."

*Well, actually you don't,* I thought to myself. I was not excited to have this guy or any guy "pray over me."

A day or two passed. I was becoming aware that these people had something I did not. They were so alive, so real, so free, so excited about God. A fire burned in them that was both captivating and a little scary. I was certain that the Holy Spirit had something to do with this and I began to realize that I wanted what they had.

Soon after this, I was alone in a little chapel late in the evening on one of the upper floors of the NET Center. Beautiful it was not. The chapel was a small, bland, square room with a musty yellow '70s-type shag carpet.

I was praying like I had never prayed before. I was pouring out my heart to God, telling him that I wanted him in my life and that I needed him. I remember saying, "God, I don't know what this baptism in the Holy Spirit thing is all about, but if you want this for me, I want it." At that very moment my life changed and it would never again be the same. There was no fanfare or trumpet blasts. Rather, I simply experienced an outpouring of God's presence that was palpable. I had heard the term "being enveloped" by God and it never made a lot of sense to me until that moment. God was so close, so real. He was there. Words can't explain what I experienced. Immediately I received various gifts of the Holy Spirit, and my life changed for good.

I am able to look at that moment and say, "There, that is when I changed. That is when God became more real to me. That is the moment that I came to understand something more about God and his Holy Spirit. At that moment I experienced freedom as I had never experienced before."

A few days later, I saw Rob again and said that I was ready to be prayed over for the baptism in the Holy Spirit. (OK, so I was a little clueless.) He gave me a strange look. "Dave, you have received it. I have seen the change in you, the way you pray, the way you worship. I don't know when it happened, but it has happened." I knew when it had happened.

Every baptized Christian needs to have such an experience. I believe that every Christian needs to be able to say, "There, that is when it happened. That is when I experienced God in a new and more profound way and he began to change my life. " I am not saying that everyone has to have the same experience that I had, nor do they have to belong to this or that movement, but God has got to move from some idea that dwells in your head to a living, personal God. We must have an encounter with God that reveals to us that he is not distant, hidden or abstract but alive and intimate. We all need to have experiences where God becomes real to us. I believe that God desires this for each and every baptized Christian. This is not something only for a select few. It is something for *you*.

Once a student asked me how he would know when this happened to him. I told him that he would just know. If you were to meet the pope, you would be darn certain that you had met him. You would not have to wonder, "Did I just meet the pope?" I believe it is the same with the Holy Spirit. You'll know.

*A Life in the Spirit*

I believe that for authentic, sustained freedom it is imperative to be living a life in the power and the anointing of the Holy Spirit. A life of freedom cannot be achieved and sustained without the power of God.

But what does it mean to "live in the Holy Spirit"? What do I mean when I speak of the "baptism of the Holy Spirit"? A good place to start is by looking at the Scriptures. Interestingly, the reference to baptism in the Holy Spirit is one of the few things that can be found in all of the Gospels as well as the Acts of the Apostles. (See Matthew 3:11; Mark 1:8; Luke 3:16; John 1:33; Acts 1:5.)

In Matthew's Gospel, John the Baptist says,

> I am baptizing you with water, for repentance, but the one who is coming after me is mightier than I. I am not worthy to carry his sandals. He will baptize you with the holy Spirit and fire. (Matthew 3:11)

Remember, John is speaking as a Jew. The Jewish people were waiting for the coming of the Spirit and for what the Spirit would bring. The prophet Ezekiel had spoken of a new heart and a new Spirit that would allow the people to walk according to God's laws (see Ezekiel 36:26–27). The prophet Isaiah had spoken of the coming of the Spirit. "I will pour water upon the thirsty ground, / and streams upon the dry land; / I will pour out my spirit upon your offspring, / and my blessing upon your descendants" (Isaiah 44:3). The prophet Joel had written, "Then afterward I will pour out / my spirit upon all mankind. / Your sons and daughters shall prophesy, / your old men shall dream dreams, / your young men shall see visions; / Even upon the servants and the handmaids, / in those days, I will pour out my spirit" (Joel 3:1–2). Clearly, references and allusions to the Holy Spirit would not have been foreign to John's audience.

So, what did John mean when he spoke of the Spirit? Well, all that I have already stated and still more. In the first chapter of Genesis, the Spirit brings order to chaos (Genesis 1:2) and in the second chapter the Spirit, who is the very breath of God, brings life. God breathed life into Adam's nostrils and allowed him to share in the divine nature of God (Genesis 2:7). That breath of God continues to give life to all of humanity. When the Spirit enters a person who is tired or worn down, the individual will experience new life.

So when John spoke of the baptism in the Holy Spirit, these would have been some of the thoughts that he evoked in his listeners, because this is where both John and his listeners were coming from. While John's baptism was a baptism of repentance, he makes it clear that this baptism of repentance will not save the people, whom he lovingly refers to as a brood of vipers. (John was a little short on tact.) Repentance is not enough (see Matthew 3:17). Instead, Jesus' baptism in the Holy Spirit is what would ultimately bring life. Just as Adam received life from the breath of God, those who received the baptism of the Holy Spirit would receive life from the Spirit of Christ. Those who were tired and weary would be given strength. To those whose lives seemed hopeless and chaotic, baptism in the Holy Spirit would bring order.

The first time I met Anna, she was totally dressed in black from head to toe. She had dyed her hair coal-black too, and if I recall correctly, her nail polish was black as well. Believe me, I don't have anything against black—it is actually my color of choice—but on a young, attractive college student, it just didn't fit.

As I got to know Anna, I realized that her preference for the color black simply expressed what was going on inside of her. When I looked into her eyes, I saw mostly black. I learned that while she was growing up, she had been moved from foster home to foster home without any sense of stability or normality. Many times she had been taken advantage of. As a result, Anna had learned that she really could not trust anyone. We began to talk occasionally, and she started to really search for God. Over time Anna opened up to God, and God broke down the walls that she had built up.

The university was sponsoring a Life in the Spirit Seminar, which is a weekend retreat focusing on the role of the Holy Spirit in a Christian's life. Anna decided to attend the retreat. The next time I saw her was on Pentecost Sunday. I was in the sanctuary of the university chapel and I was struck by what I saw. Anna was in one of the front rows in the chapel, dressed in the most beautiful simple red dress. Anna was glowing. Once again, her choice in clothing was only expressing what was going on inside of her. God is so good. Through the power of his Spirit in her, he had freed Anna from many of the things that had kept her bound.

*Saint Peter Got It...Finally*
Something very similar happened to Saint Peter. Peter is one of my favorite characters in the Bible. I am able to relate with him on many levels. Peter, in his enthusiasm and passion, often speaks without thinking. "Let's build a tent," he said, without thinking (see Mark 9:5). I too often speak without thinking. Peter was a fisherman and I too love to fish. Peter walked on water.... Well, maybe the similarities end there, but Peter is a perfect example in the Scriptures of why we need the power of the Holy Spirit in our lives if we are really going to be free.

As one of the twelve, Peter also held a special place with Jesus. He was one of the three disciples who were part of the "inner circle." Jesus called specifically for Peter, James and John at many significant events in his life. Peter saw many of Jesus' miracles. He was there when the woman with a hemorrhage was healed (see Luke 8:43–46). He was with Jesus when Bartimaeus was healed of his blindness (see Mark 10:46–52). Don't forget how Peter's own mother-in-law was healed (see Matthew 8:14–15). Peter was present when Jesus was transfigured (see Mark 9:1–7), and it was Peter who boldly proclaimed that Jesus was the Messiah, the Son of God (see Matthew 16:16). Finally, it was Peter who lamented, "Master, to whom shall we go? You have the words of eternal life" (John 6:68).

Peter was blessed to be able to walk, talk, listen and laugh with Jesus. It was Peter whom Jesus called out of the boat and invited to walk on the water. It was Peter upon whom Jesus chose to build the Church.

Finally, let's not forget that Peter was the one who stood in the empty tomb (see Luke 24:12). Imagine that. Knowing very well that Jesus had been crucified and that he had died and then hearing that Jesus had been raised made Peter run to the tomb, only to stand in the still, dark tomb "amazed" at what had happened. Peter not only saw the empty tomb, but he stood in it, and he saw that Jesus was not there.

It would seem that Peter had every possible advantage. And yet, it was Peter who, at the accusation of a little girl around a campfire, denied that he knew Jesus. Not once, but three times he stated that he did not know him.

Sadly, this would be another thing that Peter and I have in common.

Do you, like me, find yourself saying things like, "It would be easier to follow Jesus if I could see him, or touch him. If only I could have been alive when he was alive, then I would be able to follow him better"?

While this line of thinking seems to make sense, I have to be honest and say I probably would be no different from the disciples, who did see him and touch him. Even with all the advantages they had, we find Peter and the other disciples cowering in an Upper Room with all the doors locked. They were being obedient to Jesus, who had "enjoined them not to depart from Jerusalem, but to wait for 'the promise of the Father about which you have heard me speak; for John baptized with water, but in a few days you will be baptized with the holy Spirit'" (Acts 1:4–5).

They waited obediently, but fearfully and without much of an idea of what was about to happen. Then, on the day of Pentecost, "there appeared to them tongues as of fire, which parted and came to rest on each one of them. And they were all filled with the holy Spirit" (Acts 2:3–4).

After that moment when the Spirit came, Peter's life would never be the same. Peter—yes, frightened, lock-the-doors, check-them-again, I-don't-even-know-him Peter—now walked out of this locked room and stood in front of thousands of people and proclaimed:

You who are Israelites, hear these words. Jesus the Nazorean was a man commended to you by God with mighty deeds, wonders, and signs, which God worked through him in your midst, as you yourselves know. This man, delivered up by the set plan and foreknowledge of God, you killed, using lawless men to crucify him.... Therefore let the whole house of Israel know for certain that God has made him both Lord and Messiah, this Jesus whom you crucified.

Now when they heard this, they were cut to the heart, and they asked Peter and the other apostles, "What are we to do, my brothers?" Peter [said] to them, "Repent and be baptized, every one of you, in the name of Jesus Christ for the forgiveness of your sins; and you will receive the gift of the holy Spirit. (Acts 2:22–24, 36–38)

Can you picture this scene? This is the same Peter who was afraid for his life and was in hiding. Because of his encounter with the Holy Spirit, Peter was forever changed. After this experience, Peter could boldly profess his faith before thousands. Peter would no longer isolate himself or shrink away from the sight of others, but he would unflinchingly stand up for the one whom he had once betrayed.

Not only did the Holy Spirit make it possible for Peter to preach boldly, but now he could go on to heal the crippled and cast out devils. We read in the book of Acts that Peter did not even need to touch people for them to be healed, that his shadow alone was enough to heal people (see Acts 5:15). Not even Jesus did that. (Of course, Jesus did say that we would do mightier things than he had done—John 14:12). Peter, much like the prophets before him, was a changed man (see 1 Samuel 10:6–7). It is not that his time with Jesus had been unimportant; surely it was. But—and I say this with some hesitation—Peter needed Jesus and still more. Jesus knew this. That's why the Holy Spirit was sent.

For a Christian to live fully the life of God, he or she *must* be filled with the Holy Spirit. We can't live the abundant life without the Spirit. We can't follow Jesus without the Holy Spirit leading us.

Peter is a perfect example of a person who was once bound and then freed. After he received the Spirit, Peter was no longer bound to what others thought of him. No longer was he bound to the fear of dying. And, as we know, this is exactly what his fate would be. Peter would be martyred for love of Christ. Peter asked only that he not die the same way Jesus did, not because he was afraid of it, but because he felt he was not worthy to die in the same way. So Peter was crucified upside down. Peter was a free man.

*Holy Spirit, Help Me*
The Holy Spirit helps us to live life the way Jesus meant it to be lived. The Christian life is not meant to be lived in fear and it is not meant to be lived behind locked doors and it is not meant to be lived silently. Rather, it is to be lived "out there." It is living dangerously at its best. The Christian life is radical and countercultural. And in order to live that way, we need the power of Jesus' Spirit. It really is that simple.

Far too many Christians are trying to live Jesus' life without the power of God. For one reason or another, they think the Holy Spirit is not for them. Many times I have heard, "Oh, I'm not into that [the Holy Spirit]."

You've got to be kidding me. Not "into that"? How is that possible? Anybody who says this is saying that they are not "into God." These people believe that they are Christians, and yet it is not possible to live the Christian life apart from the Holy Spirit. The Scriptures say we can't even say Jesus is Lord without the power of the Holy Spirit (see 1 Corinthians 12:3). The Holy Spirit is the Third Person of the Trinity. You can't divorce the Holy Spirit from God the Father and Jesus the Son.

There is a bishop in Africa who will not ordain men who have not experienced the baptism in the Holy Spirit. "It would be wrong for me to do this," he says. "How can I expect them to do the work of Jesus if they don't have the power of Jesus?"

I know some people may be saying, "I'm not into this or that movement." Fine. Don't be a part of that movement. I am not endorsing or encouraging you to be a part of any particular movement, I am simply stressing the absolute importance of living in the anointing of God's Holy Spirit, without which I believe no Christian is able to fully live the life Christ has in mind for us.

Others may be saying, "My Aunt Mary was a part of some group that spoke a lot about the Holy Spirit and she was a nut." Probably so; I really can't argue with you. However, take that up with your aunt, not the Holy Spirit. The Holy Spirit is waiting to move in your heart and bring your faith alive. Let this happen. This isn't something that only "holy" people need. It is not something for other people. It is something you need. It is something I need every day.

It is important to note that being filled with God's Spirit is not something that simply happens once, rather it should happen over and over again. The prayer I say more often then any other is, "Come Holy Spirit." When not saying my rosary, I often simply pray, "Come Holy Spirit." I remember a priest saying that he continually asks the Holy Spirit to fill him. When asked why, Father responded, "Because I leak."

It is God's desire to pour out his Holy Spirit on us. Jesus tells us in Luke's Gospel: "If you then, who are wicked, know how to give good gifts to your children, how much more will the Father in heaven give the holy Spirit to those who ask him?" (Luke 11:13).

We only need to go before the Father, the Giver of all good gifts, and ask him to fill us with his Holy Spirit.

### It's in the Fruit

As you grow in the Holy Spirit and in freedom, people will begin to notice. Once when I was home from college visiting my parents in Arizona, most of the family was out fooling around in the pool. I was in the kitchen doing the dishes. Let it be known: I hate doing dishes. One time when I was younger, my older brothers took advantage of my religious sensitivities and persuaded me to believe that God would be pleased if I did dishes every day during Lent. I believed them, but I failed to grasp the benefit that my brothers would gain by my lenten sacrifice. Within a day or two, while I was doing dishes as they were watching TV, I realized I had been had. No doubt for that little sham they will spend extra time in purgatory doing the dishes from the banquet table in heaven. At any rate, that day in Arizona I was doing the dishes and singing some song of worship. My sister noticed, and said to our mom, "God has done something pretty amazing in Dave's life. He is in there doing the dishes without complaining, and he is singing." Believe me, if God can do that in my life, he can do anything in yours.

My older brother was also able to see it. Around this same time he stated, "Dave is finally the person he always wanted to be." My brother was correct. The Holy Spirit gave me the power and the strength to live the way I wanted to and the way I knew God wanted me to.

But what does it mean to be baptized in the Holy Spirit? Books have been written on the subject, but for me the baptism in the Holy Spirit is pretty simple. For me, the experience of the baptism in the Holy Spirit created a greater desire for God. The baptism in the Holy Spirit ultimately causes the individual to have a greater experience of the person of Jesus. Because of the baptism of the Holy Spirit, Christ ceases to be simply some historical figure and more fully becomes for us who in fact he is, the Son of the living God who came into the world, suffered and died and rose so that we may live. This is at the very heart of the baptism on the Holy Spirit.

After the baptism of the Spirit, I found that I had a greater desire to pray and a greater desire to be with God. I experienced my prayer as being much more fruitful. It was not simply me sitting in front of God getting frustrated wondering if he was there or not. It was as if he himself were so very present that sitting in his presence was enough; he didn't have to say anything. Being near him was all that I needed.

With the baptism of the Holy Spirit comes an insatiable desire for intimacy for God. Many people also experience a greater love for the Scriptures. Another fruit I have experienced is a greater love and desire for the sacraments. The Mass has come alive. It is not the music or the preaching that is the most satisfying, rather it is the Eucharist itself. The baptism of the Spirit marked the time when I started to know more deeply and profoundly that Jesus really is present in the Eucharist.

The other major effect has been a freedom over sin. Empowered with the Holy Spirit, I obtained a greater freedom from the bondage to the sin in my life that I had struggled with. This is not to say that I never sinned again. (I have, at least once!) It's just that I really have been able to root out certain sins and experience more love, joy, peace, patience, kindness, generosity, faithfulness, gentleness, self-control, patience, kindness and the other fruits of the Spirit (see Galatians 5:22–23).

So, by the power of his Holy Spirit dwelling in me, God has changed and is changing my life. As Paul states in the Second Letter to the Corinthians, I really have become a new creation (see 2 Corinthians 5:17). The Spirit of God really is a Spirit of freedom. That same Spirit wants to overwhelm you too, and lead you to freedom.

## JOURNEY TO GOD'S HEART

*Listening:*
Romans 8:13–26

*Reflecting:*
What fruit of the Spirit is evident in your life?
If you are honest with yourself, are you
afraid of the Holy Spirit?

*Conversing:*
"Holy Spirit, enlighten my mind so that I
may understand..."
"Holy Spirit come; I am tired of trying to
follow Christ on my own strength."

## CHAPTER EIGHT

## TRUE FREEDOM

WHAT IS TRUTH? PILATE WAS NOT THE FIRST PERSON TO ASK THIS question, nor will he be the last. I would guess that at one time or another everyone has asked it. I believe it's an essential question for each of us to ask and to keep asking until we're certain we have found an answer. Jesus says that the truth shall set us free (see John 8:32). If we want to be free, we had better settle the question of what truth is.

What is truth? In the film *A Few Good Men*, Jack Nicholson's character states, "You can't handle the truth!" Is he right? Can we handle the truth? Can we argue with it? Is something true simply because I believe it to be true? This is a question that is constantly being debated in our culture. History has seen the discussion of truth take on many different facets.

*Worldview*

When discussing truth I think it's important to look at the historical context or the worldview that surrounds the issue. For the sake of simplicity, let's look at the topic of worldview in three historical segments, premodern, modern and postmodern.

The premodern worldview segment runs from the beginning of time until about the 1500s. During this time the supernatural (God) dictated everything. God was in the heavens and he controlled all things—health, weather, life and death. God was everywhere and involved in everything. He was the starting point of all discussions. The purpose of science, philosophy, art, music—any area of study—was to glorify God.

During this period of time, it was believed that there were absolute truths and they could be known. Truth was assumed to be rooted in God, and it was assumed that God would reveal truth to human beings. Truth was undisputed and it was objective. The same things were true for all times and peoples and in all circumstances and situations.

By the 1600s the world was changing from the premodern world to the so-called modern world. This was the time of the Enlightenment or the Age of Reason. While God had been at the center of the premodern world, the human person was the center of the modern world. The human mind and human reason reigned supreme. It was believed that if a man simply put his mind to something, he would be able to solve any problem. Instead of believing in God unquestioningly, people chose to believe in God or not. Even those who believed that he existed began to believe that he certainly no longer had any intimate contact with the world.

Swiftly the world moved away from the idea of objective truth. The concept of a God who reveals truth became foreign. From now on, people decided, the culture or the society would determine what is true. Truth became relative, in that it depended on the times, on the society or on a certain group of people. Right and wrong were no longer based on the nature of God but on human reasoning or human wisdom. Culture would dictate what is true. Art, philosophy and science would exist to bring glory to the intellect of man rather than to God.

Eventually, problems with this worldview developed. The early part of the twentieth century was a time of tremendous upheaval, with multiple world wars and extreme evil. Something had gone terribly wrong. The human race, which was supposed to be able to make things better and solve all the world's ills, found instead that things were getting drastically worse. Something had to change.

After the Second World War, it did. The middle part of the last century ushered in a time of tremendous change, a time of transition to a worldview that is now commonly known as postmodernism.

Whereas in the premodern world God had been at the center, and in the modern world humankind or society had been at the center, in our postmodern world the *individual* is at the center. It's all about *you*. The individual is at the center of everything. Truth, no longer rooted in God or even in culture, instead emanates from each individual. No longer absolute or objective, truth has become totally relative. Now, whatever an individual believes to be true is true. The individual, in other words, is the source of his or her own truth and belief in this individual brand of truth does not need to be shared with anyone else to be valid.

One need only reflect on this for a moment in order to see this will lead to absolute confusion. The single most descriptive word for this worldview would probably be "chaos." This postmodern segment of history happens to be the time we are living in today.

*Rejection of Truth*

So then, one of the most prominent marks of postmodernism is the rejection of absolute truth. For this generation, relativism triumphs. I am sure that this is why then-Cardinal Ratzinger prayed at Pope John Paul II's funeral Mass that the world would be freed from the "tyranny of relativism." In this relativistic, postmodern world, the mantra, "what is true for me is true and what is true for you is true," reigns supreme in spite of the fact that simple logic should reveal this is not possible. How can two opposing views both be true? No wonder this mind-set has led to such tremendous turmoil.

In reality, some things are true and some things are false. I don't state that only because I believe it, but because God has ordained it this way. There is such a thing as absolute truth, defined as commandments or norms that are true for all people, at all times, in all places, even though this concept is foreign to this generation. Declaring that some things are always true for all people at all times requires individuals to assent to the idea that truth must exist outside of them, and the postmodern world simply can't do this. Statements such as this are not only alien to postmodern ears, but they must be vehemently defended against.

Contrary to the postmodern worldview, I am not, nor are you, the one who determines what truth is. Truth is objective; it is apart from me; it is rooted in God. It is essential for us to realize that *the* source of absolute truth is the One who is Absolute. The attempt to wrest the truth out of its God-anchor and to try to root it down into something other than God has led only to confusion, even bedlam. While it may appear to be liberated thinking to say that my believing something to be true makes it true, especially if I believe it passionately, it actually leads to bondage, disarray and turmoil.

Do you understand what we're dealing with? If you understand the postmodern worldview, you can get some insight into why people become so angry when you express disagreement with them or with their lifestyles. You see, if people believe that the individual is the source of what is true, but I don't acquiesce to their strongly held beliefs, then my expression of disagreement seems a lot like a personal rejection to them. Besides, the "truth" is rooted in each individual, so how dare you disagree with it?

When I express an opinion that is contrary to what another person believes to be true, I am oftentimes ridiculed or told that I am closed-minded, a bigot or, God forbid, not "tolerant." Of course, my accusers have skewed the meaning of tolerance. Traditionally, tolerance meant that I accepted the person but did not have to accept his or her beliefs or behavior. You've heard the adage, "love the sinner, not the sin." But this new definition of tolerance holds that we must not only accept the person but we must also respect—that is, believe—what they believe. This is a radical change in only the past fifty years.[1] Ironically, as it turns out, in today's world the only thing that one need *not* be tolerant toward are those peoples or institutions that believe and teach absolute truths.

Understanding this clash of worldviews can help us understand the level of emotion and anger that is often leveled against us personally or against the Church at large.

*The Truth*
This is all good to know about, but what does it have to do with freedom? Quite simply, I believe that a very significant reason many people are not free is that they live much of their lives believing what is not true. Lies or untruths have permeated the way they think, what they believe and how they act. This means that their "houses" are built on sand instead of on the Rock (see Matthew 7:24–27). Sand is unstable. A life of instability and uncertainty is a life filled with worries and turmoil, and the end result is death.

Clearly and authoritatively, Jesus says that he is the truth (see John 14:6) and that truth will set us free (see John 8:32). If I desire to know what is true and to be free, then it is absolutely essential that I come to know Christ, who is the source of truth and freedom. When we are in Christ we come to recognize what is not true and this helps free us from our darkness.

Here's the problem, though: If I don't know that I am in the dark and I don't realize that I have believed lies, how can I turn to Jesus to be freed from my bondage? Believing that something is true makes me unaware that it's a lie. My whole life may be affected, but I don't realize why. A good example of this is the student who believes his parents' divorce is his fault. Having believed this since he was a little boy, he thinks it's true, even though believing it holds him in tremendous bondage and riddles him with guilt. He has just gotten used to it; he's not aware that it's a false belief. His parents' divorce was in truth not his fault, of course. But thinking that it was his fault has been a part of his belief system for so long that he has simply come to accept it as being true. He needs God's light to shine into his darkness, so that he can walk free from the trap of this untruth.

Without God's help, we continue to "live a lie." Another example is the young woman who sat in my office explaining to me how it was her fault that she was raped. "I should have not gone on a date with him...should not have been alone...." Her story went on. This young woman truly believed that it was her fault that the terrible offense happened to her. She was "living a lie." Because of this she punished herself for what had happened. She began to believe that she would never be able to have a healthy, holy relationship with a man. She believed that she was "dirty" and that no one really wonderful would ever care for her because of what had been done to her. It wasn't until we prayed that she would know God's truth that she began to see that what she was believing was not true. Slowly, with God's help, she began to be free from the burden of the lies that had paralyzed her for so long.

So you see, the closer we get to the Light the more we are able to see into the darkness. As we are drawn into the Truth, the more we become aware of what is not true, so that we can allow ourselves to become conformed to the Truth. This is why it is so essential that we allow our very beings to be consumed by God.

As a prayer exercise, I often have people simply pray for light. I invite them to pray before God who is light and imagine them being enveloped in this light (see 1 John 1:5). Oftentimes this simple exercise produces very powerful fruit. Misbeliefs to which individuals were blind slowly begin to appear, and in God's consuming love, the lies burn away.

If you can identify the lies that are hiding in the nooks and crannies of your mind and heart, you can submit them to God and you can go free. If you are not able to identify the lies, you will continue to be controlled by them and you will not be able to be fully free. You will continue to live out of the lies and to make choices from a place of untruth rather than a place of truth.

The stories are almost endless.... The young man who feels like he is never going to make anything of himself because he was always disappointing his dad. Or the woman who never feels beautiful because her father never told her that she was. Or the woman who believes if she could just lose five more pounds everything would be wonderful. The lies go on and on. In the name of freedom, they have to be stopped.

Jim was another victim of lies. When Jim was a young boy, another boy in his neighborhood sexually abused him. Jim was ashamed of what had happened and, as is typical, became convinced that something was wrong with *him*. Because of his shame about the incident, he vowed that no one would ever find out about it. He assumed that if anyone ever found out he would be ridiculed and made fun of and he would not be able to live with himself. Jim lived his life in a cocoon for fear that someone would find out his secret. He recalls how once in high school, he was in class and a group of guys was laughing about something. He was certain that they were laughing about what had happened to him, so in the middle of class he started a fight with them. Jim was continually getting into trouble like that. Eventually, he developed an addiction to drugs and alcohol to help dull his pain.

After years of difficulties, Jim met someone who began to evangelize him. Jim came to know the Lord. Slowly he began to know the truth. At last he could see that the abuse was not his fault and that other people were not at all aware of what had happened to him and that he had no reason to be ashamed. Most importantly, he did not have to hide his secret from the world. He slowly began to realize that people would still love and care for him even if they did hear what had happened to him. Jim even shared his testimony with a group of young people. He shared his story and gave testimony to God's truth and the freedom that it brings. Once the light of Christ began to shine in his mind and heart, he began to know what was true. This, in turn, set him free.

*Not My Word*

As I pray with people, there have been numerous occasions when I knew that they were simply bound by a lie. People probably get tired of hearing me say, "But the truth is...." But my statement alone is not enough to set someone free. I can tell someone what is true and the person may be able to look at the situation and agree with me. However, twenty minutes later, the person will probably still believe the same old lie. Even if the individual decides to repeat a mantra to remind himself or herself of what is true (which may be a good idea), it almost never leads to real, sustained freedom. I can tell someone a million times what is true but so often the lies are so deep and so pervasive that my repetition has no lasting effect.

I can't set you free. You can't free yourself. Even repeating the truth can't set you free. Only the Son can set you free (remember John 8:36). It is fine for me to tell someone what is true, but how much more powerful is it when the same individual hears the truth from Jesus himself. His word sets us free, and he gives us the grace we need to walk in our new freedom. When one is able to present oneself to Jesus and is able to hear him counter the lie with a word of truth, well, there is *real* freedom. The lies that have caged us for so long crumble in the presence of the Truth. We no longer have to live in shadows and darkness but can bask in the light of God's freedom.

## JOURNEY TO GOD'S HEART

*Listening:*
Psalm 25

*Reflecting:*
Think about your worldview and see if you
can discern postmodern influences.
Consider, with God's help, where you may
have believed a lie, or more than one lie.

*Conversing:*
"Lord, help me to be more honest
with you and myself."
"Jesus, shine your truth into my
heart and reveal the lies. What word of
truth do you want to speak to my heart?"

## CHAPTER NINE

## FREEDOM TO WORSHIP

I THINK I HAVE PRAYED EVERY DAY THAT I CAN REMEMBER. WHEN I was younger, it may have only been a very short, simple prayer before I went to bed, but I always felt that it was very important to pray each day. I must admit that there were times when I was in high school that I lay in bed saying my prayers with the room spinning. Clearly, I was missing something. (I am so grateful for Psalm 25:7: "Remember no more the sins of my youth; / remember me only in light of your love.")

One time, I think when I was still in high school, I was getting ready for bed, and I stated firmly to God that I did not *feel* like praying. Instantly, it seemed as if God said to me, "And I didn't *feel* like dying on the cross." Point taken. I fell to my knees and said my prayers. God is able to make his point very clearly.

In the life of a Christian, prayer is not an option. And if you want to be free, you must pray. Being transformed and freed by him does not happen by mere chance; it is the fruit of a decision to develop a lifestyle of prayer. Prayer is not simply a duty, it is one of the primary ways to approach God and to have him help us find our way in the world in which we live.

That being said, prayer is difficult. This is probably why so many of the saints called it "the discipline." What is probably most important, therefore, if you are going to grow in your prayer life (and note I said "prayer life" not "prayer moment"), is that you *begin*. There has to be a beginning, a certain day when you decide that you are going to be a person of prayer and you begin to pray. I know you are busy. I know you have screaming children hanging on you seventeen hours a day. I know that you work far more hours than you should. Believe me—I have probably heard just about every reason *not* to begin a prayer life. My guess is I have used most of them myself. Some are more creative than others, but all of them are stumbling blocks that must be overcome.

On the other side of the coin, I have also heard from the people who say they "pray at all times." These people do not have a specific time, because, they say, "I am praying always." Although this is edifying, you still need some time each day when you get away from everything so you can sit and be still before God. You must find a time that you can set apart for God alone. So here is what you need to do.

Ready?

Listening?

*Start.*

It's that simple, just start. This is one time where I actually agree with the ad slogan, "Just do it!" Prayer is like so many other things in our lives. The more we do it, the better we get. Prayer is easier for some and more difficult for others. Some people are naturally more gifted at prayer while others have to work much harder. But what is essential at the beginning is that you just start.

There, you have started a life of prayer. Of course, there are things you can do that enable you to pray better, but the most important thing is that you simply begin, that you take time to pray. Prayer isn't only up to you, it is also the work of God. But it takes your cooperation as well.

When you are first beginning to pray, it is important to have realistic expectations. Don't expect yourself to begin with an hour of contemplation every day. Begin with what you think is reasonable after reflecting and praying about it. You should try to move toward taking time each day, but at the beginning even this may not be possible. Perhaps you need to start with fifteen minutes a day a couple of times a week. That is a great start. Begin there, and if you find you need more time, then take it. At the beginning it is important to set yourself up to succeed.

More often than not, the problem I see is people trying to take on too much. When they don't do well, then they get discouraged and frustrated and things begin to unravel. Keep it simple. Simple beginnings are most important.

After many years of offering spiritual direction, I am generally most impressed with the person who is faithful to fifteen minutes of praying *every* day. Some people start out of the blocks really well ("I prayed two hours today!"), but quickly fade. This is a marathon, not a sprint. Pace yourself.

One more thing: If on a given day you are not able to pray don't say, "I will pray double tomorrow." This only leads to trouble. Before too long you will "owe" God 3,430 minutes. Each day, begin anew; I don't believe God looks at your life in twenty-four-hour segments.

There are literally thousands of books and articles written on how to help you pray better, so I don't really want to spend a lot of time on the basic "how to." Very briefly, let's take a look at what Jesus says about prayer, so we can get an idea of how to pray:

> He was praying in a certain place, and when he had finished, one of his disciples said to him,
> "Lord, teach us to pray just as John taught his disciples." He said to them, "When you pray, say:
> Father, hallowed be your name,
>    your kingdom come.
> Give us each day our daily bread
> and forgive us our sins
> for we ourselves forgive everyone in
>    debt to us,
> and do not subject us to the final
>    test." (Luke 11:1–4)

When the disciples asked Jesus to teach them to pray, they were really saying, "Teach us to pray like you were just praying. We want to do it like you do." And Jesus begins with "Father." Prayer is all about relationship. Everything you do in prayer flows from this first word, *Father*. "God, you are Father, I am your son. You are protector; I need your protection. You are healer; I need to be healed. You are the one who frees; I need to be freed." At the very beginning of your prayer, establish the relationship that will guide your prayer.

Note that Jesus' first word was not "Santa." This is important, because I think many of us pray as if God is really Santa Claus. We get this idea that God is watching to see if we are good or bad, and we get good things if we behave. We sit on his lap, and we do most of the talking, which usually involves asking for things.

So begin your prayer with "Father," and affirm his holiness. Spend some time just gazing on God's beauty. "Father, you are holy, and I am going to simply be in your presence and allow your goodness to overwhelm me."

Ask God to give you what you will need that day. Don't ask for bread for the rest of your living days; trust that he will be with you tomorrow and he will feed you then as well. Ask to be forgiven from sins of the past and to be protected from transgressions of the future. That's it. I believe that all of our prayer can be summed up in this. Jesus was giving his followers a pattern for how to pray. It was what he did and he invites us to do it the same way.

There are a few very practical things that may help. You need to have a place where you can be quiet, where you are comfortable and where you will be uninterrupted. It is great if you are able to pray in a chapel somewhere but not everyone is able to do this. If you are praying in your home, something has to be different when you pray. When I pray in my room in the friary I have an oil lamp that I light. The only time I light this is when I am praying. It is a very simple ritual, but when I light that lamp I know the time is different. It is set aside; it is prayer.

When I am done praying, I blow it out and my prayer is finished. This very simple action makes a normal space and time holy.

One more thing: Don't forget to be quiet. This is probably the most essential point, and the one most often skipped. It is difficult, because we are not accustomed to being silent. I don't mean not talking, I mean being silent. When your prayer begins to move from your head to your heart, when prayer is not so much about "thinking" but about being, it is at this place that our prayer begins to really shape who we are and who we are going to become. And this type of prayer takes work and it takes practice. I would love to say that I am able to be really quiet every time I pray, but that is not the case. Sometimes I have so many things going on inside of my head that I just can't break through. But that is OK. For me one of the most important things (and I think God delights in this) is that I am there. There have been so many times when I have been in prayer for an hour and I wonder if I really prayed at all. But I whisper to God, "at least I am here," and I like to think he smiles. Prayer so often for me is just making myself available. "Here I am, Father..." and sometimes that's all I've got to say.

*Praying for Freedom*
So what I'm saying is that you need to pray. Don't worry if you are doing it perfectly or not. Make the time soon and begin to pray.

When I pray, it is not about gaining or gathering stuff. I am not trying to recharge my spiritual batteries. While this does at times happen, it is a fruit and is not the main focus. For me the spiritual life of prayer is not about getting or building up, but rather it is about emptying and getting rid of. Prayer is about being freed from whatever it is that binds us.

Philippians 2:6–11 is called the *kenotic* text. *Kenosis* is a Greek word that means, "self-emptying" and this text speaks of Jesus emptying himself and becoming like us:

> Have among yourselves the same attitude that is also yours in Christ Jesus,
>> Who, though he was in the form of God,
>> did not regard equality with God
>>> something to be grasped.
>> Rather, he emptied himself,
>> taking the form of a slave,
>> coming in human likeness;
>> and found human in appearance,
>> he humbled himself,
>> becoming obedient to death,
>>> even death on a cross. (Philippians 2:5–8)

I believe this *kenosis* is central to our praying for and experiencing of freedom. We need to empty ourselves of ourselves. I will readily admit that it is a frightening prayer to say, "Jesus, allow me to be empty, strip me of everything that is not of you so that I may be truly free." What we are praying is that God would take away everything that is not of him so that the only thing that remains is God himself. This is true freedom.

We spend too much time in our prayer holding on to things. If we can actually begin to be comfortable with letting go and being stripped empty, our prayer lives and spiritual lives change radically. Instead of expending so much energy trying to keep everything together, plugging the holes in the dike with every finger and toe, it may be best to let the dam break. Then we can stop propping everything up and allow ourselves to be exposed before God. Then our lives really do change.

It's crazy, but so often when we pray we try to pretend to be something that we are not. Do we think God is impressed? It is a freeing experience when we can come before God just as we are without trying to put on airs. Just let God do what he needs to do in us. Saint Francis said, "What we are before God is what we are and nothing else." And get this: *That's enough.* This really is good news. God delights in us just as we are.

If I can be more detached in my prayer life, if surrender really can be normative for me, then I can experience a freedom that really can't be taken away. To be able to be detached is such an amazingly freeing experience. Does this make sense? Can you visualize it? When you are stripped, emptied or detached there is nothing for you to hold on to, so nothing can be taken away. Detached from everything else, all we have is God, and he is enough. Again, it was Saint Francis who said, "Oh God, you are enough for me." He did not say, "God, you are everything." I have met many people who had everything and it was not enough. On the other hand, I have met men and women who had nothing and were satisfied. Imagine how free you would be if you could echo Francis' prayer, "Oh God, you are enough for me."

Just so that I am clear here: I am not really talking about things like cars, houses and that kind of stuff. Granted, it is important to be able to give God these things so that you do not have an inordinate attachment to them. But here I am talking about being stripped and detached and becoming empty of all the things I have spoken about up to this point, such as fear, anger, hatred, envy, greed, hurt and addictions. These are the trappings I am talking about. When we pray that our hearts can be emptied of all of these things, we experience freedom in our prayer.

For many people one of the greatest sources of bondage is the past, particularly past sins. This too must be surrendered to God. Your past is just that, past. It should not bind your present or limit your future. As soon as you are able to give God your yesterdays, your tomorrows can be filled with grace and freedom. Some of the greatest saints had the most checkered pasts, but they were able to give God their past experiences and move on. And so must you.

*Hope and Freedom*

Studies show that the human body can live about two weeks without eating any food. If we go without water, we can only survive for a couple of days. I believe we can live but a mere moment without hope. Hope gives life. I know there are times on our journey when we feel as if we really can walk no further and the virtue of hope is the only thing that allows us to go on. One of my very favorite Scriptures is from Isaiah 40:31: "They that hope in the LORD will renew their strength, / they will soar as with eagles' wings; / They will run and not grow weary, / walk and not grow faint."

If you are going to really understand and live this text, there is one point that you need to be absolutely sure about. Freedom is only possible if your hope is in the Lord. If you are going to truly be happy and truly free, your hope must be in God and in God alone. The problem is that we can place our hope in lots of other things. Many of them are really wonderful things, but they are not God and they ultimately bind us and do not lead to life.

When I was about five years old, my mother was diagnosed with multiple sclerosis (MS). I remember the evening I learned my mom had MS. Mom was in the hospital and the rest of the family had gathered in our living room. My dad was with me and my four brothers and my sister and he read a letter to us from my mom. What I recall the letter basically saying was that my mom was sick but that she was going to be OK and that God would help us. As a kid I did not really understand what was going on but I remember my dad and my older brothers and sister being upset, and this frightened me.

My mom's MS really bothered me. I didn't understand why such a wonderful person had to have something like that happen to her. I would often pray that God would heal her of her MS, but he never did. At times I would get so frustrated that I would get mad, but it never seemed to make any difference; her MS never went away. Much, much later I realized that in some respect I had placed my hope in my mom's MS being cured. I realized that as long as I did this I could never really be free. I would be bound to frustration, anger and, at times, hurt, because she wasn't healed.

Your hope must be in the Lord and in the Lord alone. Would it have been a wonderful event for my mom to be healed of MS? Of course, but if my hope was dependent on that outcome, I would continually be disappointed. I am sure that you spend a great deal of time praying for wonderful things, and there is nothing wrong with that. But your hope cannot be rooted in that prayer being answered the way *you* think is best. It would be great if your husband's cancer were healed or your father's Alzheimer's were treatable. I agree that it would be a blessing if all of your children would return to the Church. However, for reasons I will never understand, some of our deepest desires, no matter how good and virtuous they are, don't turn out the way we want. This is why our hope cannot be in those things.

I have dealt with so many people who are angry with God because their prayers did not get answered the way they wanted. For many of them, this causes a significant faith crisis. "Why wouldn't God want this?" I can't answer that. But I know that unless you are able to place your hope in Christ and in Christ alone you will never be truly happy or free. You must be able to become detached even from these things, as good and wonderful as they are, and give God all your hope. If you are able to do this, there is no doubt that you will experience greater freedom.

This does not mean we stop praying for our loved ones or that we make ourselves in some way devoid of any desire for them to be healed. It is just that when it is all said and done, our hope needs to lie in God alone. This will not be shaken.

Prayer will sustain you. As I have mentioned several times, a life of prayer is difficult, but as my dad always said, anything worthwhile always is. It is a tremendous comfort knowing that God desires to have a relationship with me and that this relationship will be developed through my prayer life. I don't always pray as well as I can or as faithfully as I should. But I do know that this is something that God has called me to and I trust that he will meet me when I reach out to him. It is in prayer that you will be able to hear God's gentle voice calling you to something more. It is when you are praying that you will be able to see his light enveloping you and transforming you. And it is in prayer that you will be able to take his hand and allow him to lead you to freedom.

### JOURNEY TO GOD'S HEART

*Listening:*
Jeremiah 29:11–15

*Reflecting:*
Why is it so difficult for you to pray?
Do you know someone who has a strong prayer life?
Talk to that person about it.

*Conversing:*
"Lord, I have always wanted to tell you..."
"Lord, I believe you want to tell me..."

## CHAPTER TEN

# FREEDOM FOR

WHAT DOES IT LOOK LIKE TO LIVE IN FREEDOM? I THINK THAT IS A really hard question because there are so many possibilities. That's like asking what a beautiful sunset looks like. There are so many different kinds. Freedom does not look only one way. What I do know is that living in freedom is *not* walking around like a Pollyanna, whistling as everything is caving in around us. It doesn't mean that we ignore the fact that really bad and difficult things happen. It doesn't mean that you ignore the pain you experience when your teenage son tells you his girlfriend is pregnant. Living in freedom doesn't mean that you will be impervious to any anxiety when you are laid off at work.

It's OK if you have a bad day. Bad days are just a part of life. Bad days do not mean that you are slipping or that God really has not worked in your life. Many times, I have people come to me frustrated because they have been struggling. For some reason they thought that once they chose freedom in Christ, they would never struggle again. This is just not realistic. We all have bad days or find that we are "down" for one reason or another. It is not the end of the world and you do not have to start all over again.

Living in freedom means keeping these things in perspective. In the midst of everything, you know that God is still sovereign, that he is holy and that he will not abandon you, no matter how crazy things become around you. Regardless of what is taking place, you do not have to lose your freedom; you do not have to fall into captivity again.

Paul said to the Galatians, "For freedom Christ set us free; so stand firm and do not submit again to the yoke of slavery" (Galatians 5:1). The victory has been won. Christ has conquered your sin and death and you are free. Now you get to spend the rest of your life basking in the glory of God's freedom. Although you don't have to fall into captivity again, sadly, many people do "submit again to the yoke of slavery."

Some of the most graphic lines in the Bible point this out well:

> What is expressed in the true proverb has happened to them, "The dog returns to its own vomit," and "A bathed sow returns to wallowing in the mire." (2 Peter 2:22; see also Proverbs 26:11)

Now, I didn't write it but I wish I had, because it captures this idea so well. Why would a dog do this? I am not even going to offer a guess, but they do. But we aren't dogs, and we should know better. We should not fall into the same trap as that of the Israelites and forget what God has done for us. We need to pray for the grace to never go back to the place of captivity, to never be yoked to slavery again. We may allow this to happen because it is so familiar. Like a mirage in the middle of the desert, the old way seems like a place of safety. However, we must recognize our tendency to return to old ways of thinking and behaving and resist them.

Recall what the disciples did after Jesus had risen but before he had ascended to his Father. They were at a loss at what to do without Jesus. Finally Peter blurted out, "I am going fishing" (John 21:3). He and the others decided to do what was familiar to them—fishing. (No one should be surprised that they did not catch anything; from my experience this seems often to be the case.) Then Jesus returned and, always so patient, took Peter aside and told him that he must now go to feed his sheep (see John 21:15–17). Peter's days of fishing for fish were now over.

There are going to be times when you feel lost and you don't know what to do or where to go. You are going to wonder where Jesus is and question if he has forgotten you. You will have a desire to just "go fishing," but you must resist this. At those times, you need to slip away and seek shelter in the Lord. Call to mind the good things God has done for you and rest with him awhile. The prophet Tobit states it well:

> Thank God! Give him the praise and the glory. Before all the living, acknowledge the many good things he has done for you, by blessing and extolling his name in song. Before all men, honor and proclaim God's deeds, and do not be slack in praising him. (Tobit 12:6)

As we have reflected, our living in freedom is not an accident; it did not just happen. God has gone to tremendous lengths in order to make us free and freedom has been purchased for us at a tremendous price. Our part is to choose to live free on a daily (and at times an hourly) basis. We have got to be able to choose freedom even when everything around us, everything in this world, is telling us it is not possible.

*Freedom for a Purpose*
One day as I was praying, I had an image of many, many people running around in a beautiful field dotted with multicolored spring flowers. The people in the scene were joyful and free. The scene was pleasant enough, but it left me feeling empty, which seemed odd. Isn't it true that my desire is to see men and women come to experience freedom? Of course; this is my prayer. But that hard-won freedom is not simply given to us so that we can run and play in a field of wildflowers. That would make us like the fifth-grader bursting gleefully out of the confines of school on the last day of class soon to be found sitting in his room, bored, asking, "Now what?" OK, I am free, but very quickly, believe it or not, gallivanting in a stunning field is not going to cut it. There has to be more than this, as good as playing in that field can be. You and I have been freed for something greater. We have been freed to love.

Pope John Paul II stated, "Freedom is made for love. If it is not used, if it does not profit from love, it becomes precisely something negative and gives us a sense of emptiness and unfulfilment."[1] If a man or woman who claims to be free does not express his or her freedom to love, I would question the authentic freedom of such a person. Of course any of us is free to act in this way but, as has already been stated, authentic freedom always wills the good of another; it does not remain strictly concerned with self.

So, is that it? Is that the sole purpose of freedom? Freedom to love?

Can you think of something greater? Go ahead and give me some wine with my cheese, but what the world really does need is love. And the person who experiences freedom, God's freedom, is in a place to offer the world what it so desperately needs. We are able to do this, we are able to love, because we have experienced freedom from everything that impedes love, and we have come to know the author of freedom. We recall that it is because he has loved us first that we are able to love (see 1 John 4:19).

Can you see a cycle developing? We experience a taste of freedom. Because of that, we are able to love a little more. When we love more, we experience greater freedom. And so the cycle goes. Obviously we see this most perfectly lived out in Jesus. But we can also see it in the many men and women who have gone before us.

I am reminded of Saint Francis of Assisi, who had a repulsion toward lepers. If Francis saw a leper coming near, he would walk the other way. But on one occasion, Francis saw a leper coming his way and, rather than running, he submitted to grace and reached out and embraced the leper and then went on his way. When he looked back on the path, however, the leper was no longer there. Francis realized it had been Christ himself, and he spent much of the rest of his days ministering to lepers. By his simple act of love and embracing the leper the first time, Francis was freer to love others.

Many others have set examples of acts of love that resulted in more freedom and further surrender, such as Mother Teresa, who lovingly bathed the poorest of poor, or Maximilian Kolbe, who offered his life for a fellow prisoner. These faithful women and men have motivated countless others to respond in much the same manner.

Our freedom, therefore, must beget love. Our acts of love spawn more freedom for ourselves and also for others, and this is lived out in the very simple, humble daily circumstances of our everyday life. It means you become more patient with your spouse, and less critical. It means taking a few extra minutes each day with your son or daughter to talk. It may mean taking ten minutes and calling the brother or sister you haven't spoken with for a long time.

Your freedom to love may oblige you to not speak or gossip about the employee that everyone in the office sees as an easy target. It may require that you be more generous with the finances with which you have been blessed. Your freedom to love may compel you and your family to volunteer at a food bank or a homeless shelter once a month. Regardless of how God will have you live out your freedom, I know without a doubt that it will involve loving others.

Jesus loved us freely and without counting the cost, and he invites us to participate with him in loving. We can't love on our own, but are able to love because Christ provides the grace for us. Jesus said, "love one another as I love you" (John 15:12).

*It's Contagious*

I walked into my office one afternoon singing one of my favorite worship songs. My secretary asked me, "How can you be so happy?" It's easy: Cleopatra is not the only Queen of Denial.

Joyously, but seriously—people notice freedom. There is something perceptible about the person who is free. When you begin to live in greater freedom, expect people to ask you what has happened. Friends around you will notice that something is different and they will mention it to you. Some will joke about it, some will be inquisitive, others will actually be frustrated. But they will notice, I guarantee it. Be ready to share with them what has taken place in your life. Saint Peter wrote that we need to "[a]lways be ready to give an explanation to anyone who asks you for a reason for your hope" (1 Peter 3:15). Be prepared to tell what God has done for you. It does not have to be some drawn-out theological explanation. Rather, simply make sure you are able to explain how God freed you and where you were when it happened. Allow him to do the rest.

This really is important because the way we live in freedom can give others permission to live freely as well. It can tell the people in your parish, your fellow soccer moms or your fishing buddies that there really is another way of living. You should be excited to tell others about this. Like a newly engaged college student, you should be prepared to tell the whole world what has happened. Don't worry if you don't know all of the answers. All you have to know is what God has done for you.

*The Road Home*

This is, of course, only the beginning. We are just starting on the road to freedom. I hope that this does not come as a surprise to you. I know we all want to be free and we hunger and thirst for more. But this freedom and joy we now experience is just a delectable appetizer of what it will be like when we finish the race. "What eye has not seen, and ear has not heard, / and what has not entered the human heart, / what God has prepared for those who love him" (1 Corinthians 2:9).

I like to think that I have a pretty good imagination, but I cannot imagine what it will be like to be in the presence of God with all of the saints and angels. What joy to be able to see God as he fully is. How comfortable to be in his presence without feeling as if I need to hide or that I have done something wrong. What *freedom* to be able to walk with him hand-in-hand.

What a moment it will be to hear God say those first words to you once again, "You are free. Well done, good and faithful servant." Ah, how sweet it will be.

It was my last week of work at Children's Hospital. I only had about three days left, and I was almost home free for my summer break. Plans never seem to work out the way I expect. I received a call from the hospital, which surprised me because I wasn't on call. The staff knew I lived closest to the hospital, so they had called me. Apparently God wanted me to learn one more thing.

Hannah was twelve years old but had never taken a single step, had never sat up, had never fed herself and had never spoken a single word. She was the size of a normal twelve-year-old, but due to a problem at birth she had never developed mentally or physically. Twelve years earlier, at the suggestion of her doctors, Hannah's parents had taken her home so that she could die there. Now, after hundreds of trips to doctors and hospitals, Hannah was once again in the hospital with multiple infections. It looked like she was not going to live through the night this time.

When I entered the waiting room, the mother asked me why God was doing this. I told her I did not know. We went on to talk and Hannah's parents told me how she had changed their lives. They shared with me about how Hannah would laugh when they placed her on the bed and bounced her up and down. "She would smile from ear to ear; she just loved that."

They wanted me to know that they were not very "religious," "but we loved her with all of our hearts." They explained how Hannah had taught them to love. "Without ever speaking a single word, Hannah taught us love. She taught us that we needed to put others first, how to sacrifice and how to care. She taught us how to take joy in the simplest things." Something told me this couple was much more religious than most religious people I have met.

"All I ever wanted is for Hannah to be able to do what all the other little girls were able to do. I wanted her to run, to laugh and to be able to play in a field. That's all I ever wanted," declared her mother.

She eventually asked me if I would pray with Hannah before I left the hospital and if I could be present when Hannah died. I promised I would try. I prayed with Hannah and one of the nurses noted with amazement how much the parents loved their little girl even though she had never really done anything for them. I informed her that she could not be more wrong; Hannah had taught them to love.

The next day I returned from Mass to find a note on my door. I was to get to the hospital as soon as possible. However, I was too late. As I stepped into Hannah's room, her mom was holding Hannah's hand with tears running down her cheeks. She looked at me with a brightness in her eyes that was not present the previous night. "Dave, she is playing. Finally, she is playing." Hannah was free.

"You are free." The words of our loving God echo through the hills and valleys of your life. Through the good times as well as the times of pain and suffering God's word to you rings true. It has always been the desire of God's heart that you live in his freedom. Today you get a taste, but one day you will drink fully of the freedom prepared for you from the beginning of time. Bless God, you are free.

## JOURNEY TO GOD'S HEART

*Listening:*
1 Corinthians 9:23–26

*Reflecting:*
Today, how can you choose to love?
Try it: Imagine what God has in store for you.

*Conversing:*
"Lord, I think that the most difficult thing
about living free will be..."
"Lord, the greatest thing about living free will be..."

# Notes

INTRODUCTION

1. From the homily of the Holy Father John Paul II, Apostolic Pilgrimage to Lourdes, Sunday, August 15, 2004, www.wff.org/JPII_LourdesHomily.html.

CHAPTER ONE: FREEDOM IS

1. From the remarks of Holy Father John Paul II to the Youth Gathering at the Kiel Center, St. Louis, Missouri, January 26, 1999. Full text can be found on the Web site of the United States Conference of Catholic Bishops at: http://www.usccb.org/pope/youth2.htm.

CHAPTER TWO: FREEDOM FIRST

1. This comment by Cardinal Christoph Schönborn can be found on the Web at www.stephanscom.at/edw/karechesen/articles/2005/12/02/a9719/.

CHAPTER SIX: FREEDOM'S GATEWAY

1. Pope John Paul II, *Words of Certitude: Excerpts from his talks and writings as Bishop and Pope* (New York: Paulist, 1979), p. 24.

CHAPTER EIGHT: TRUE FREEDOM

1. See Josh McDowell, *Right from Wrong* (Nashville: Thomas Nelson, 1994) and *The New Tolerance* (Carol Stream, Ill.: Tyndale, 1998).

CHAPTER TEN: FREEDOM FOR

1. Pope John Paul II, *Love and Responsibility* (San Francisco: Ignatius, 1993), p. 135.

4/4th Tuesday.